I0888181

(A SHORT ACCOUNT OF) ENGLAND'S FOREIGN TRADE IN THE NINETEENTH CENTURY

(A SHORT ACCOUNT OF) ENGLAND'S FOREIGN TRADE IN THE NINETEENTH CENTURY

Its economic and social results

ARTHUR L. BOWLEY

Routledge
Taylor & Francis Group
LONDON AND NEW YORK

First published in 1893

Published 2006 by Routledge
2 Park Square, Milton Park, Abingdon, Oxfordshire OX14 4RN
711 Third Avenue, New York, NY 10017

First issued in paperback 2014

Routledge is an imprint of the Taylor and Francis Group, an informa business

British Library Cataloguing in Publication Data
A CIP catalogue record for this book
is available from the British Library

(A Short Account of) England's Foreign Trade in the Nineteenth Century
ISBN 0-415-38226-2 (volume)
ISBN 0-415-37978-4 (subset)
ISBN 0-415-28619-0 (set)

ISBN 13: 978-1-138-86528-0 (pbk)
ISBN 13: 978-0-415-38226-7 (hbk)

Routledge Library Editions: Economic History

DIAGRAM I

General view of the Foreign Trade of the United Kingdom in the XIXth Centy

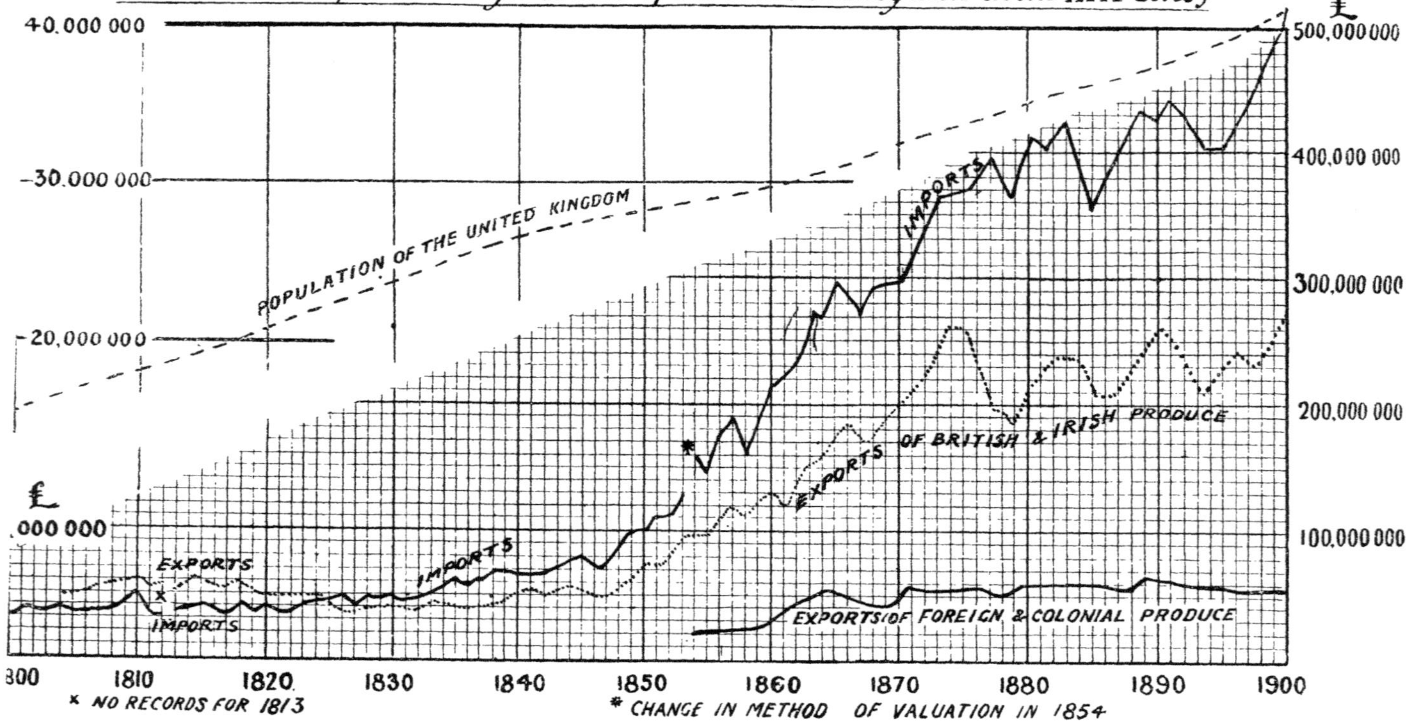

A SHORT ACCOUNT OF

ENGLAND'S FOREIGN TRADE

IN THE NINETEENTH CENTURY

ITS ECONOMIC AND SOCIAL RESULTS

BY

ARTHUR L. BOWLEY, M.A.

Cobden Prizeman (Cambridge), 1892;
Formerly Scholar of Trinity College, Cambridge.

WITH TEN STATISTICAL DIAGRAMS

REVISED EDITION

"Here shall you trace in flowing operation,
In every state of practical busy movement,
The rills of civilisation."
—WALT WHITMAN.

LONDON
SWAN SONNENSCHEIN & CO., LIM.
NEW YORK: CHARLES SCRIBNER'S SONS
1905

FIRST EDITION, *October*, 1893.
SECOND EDITION, *June*, 1905.

PREFACE

THE subject set for the essay for the Cobden Prize awarded at Cambridge University in December, 1892, was "Changes in the Volume, Character, and Geographical Distribution of England's Foreign Trade in the Nineteenth Century, and their Causes." The essay which was then successful was not published at once, but has been re-cast and completed, while additions and changes have been made to bring it within the scope of the "Social Science Series."

As it now stands, it does not profess to be a complete account of our recent foreign trade—that being of course impossible in a book of this size, where the subject of each chapter would easily fill a volume by itself; but an endeavour has been made to point out and give the right prominence to the more important of the events and causes that have affected the growth of trade, to touch on the more obvious of the social effects of this growth, and more especially to furnish an introductory text-book, which will supply the fundamental facts of this century's commerce in an easily accessible form.

Tables of figures have been as far as possible

avoided, since they are liable merely to weary the reader without affording him any real information, but their place is supplied by diagrams, on the use of which it is desired to lay special stress. By these it is possible to present at a glance all the facts which could be obtained from figures as to the increase, fluctuations, and relative importance of prices, quantities, and values of different classes of goods and trade with various countries; while the sharp irregularities of the curves give emphasis to the disturbing causes which produce any striking change. In many cases, perhaps, more can be learnt by considering and accounting for all the features of a diagram than in any other way, so that the text of this book may to some extent be regarded as an explanation and interpretation of the plates. Great care has been taken to ensure the accuracy of these; they are substantially the same as those sent with the original essay to the Vice-Chancellor, but have all been redrawn and verified.

A. L. B.

BRISTOL,
5th September, 1893.

NOTE TO REVISED EDITION, 1905.

IN this edition the tables and diagrams have been continued to 1903, and errors and misprints have been corrected throughout. As the original edition was stereotyped, it has not been possible to introduce any alteration of treatment or arrangement, and the book is still substantially that published in 1894. It should be understood that the author does not feel bound to support every opinion he advanced at that date, in some cases on subjects to which he has given no further attention. It is hoped, however, that the great part of the book depends on facts, not on opinions, and that, with the few amendments that friendly criticism has shown to be necessary, these are correctly stated. Since the first edition, the policy of Free Trade has been attacked, and all tariff questions have become controversial; statements which were commonplace in 1893 will in 1905 appear to be dogmatic. It seemed impossible to alter the treatment of this subject without embarking on a long historical and controversial analysis, and therefore the paragraphs relating to Free Trade and Imperial relations have been left untouched. It is perhaps important to notice that in a book emanating from Cambridge ten years ago, many of the arguments recently brought forward by tariff reformers were, however lightly, indicated and summarised. (See pp. 15, 16, 41-46, 123-4.) The arguments that filled the newspapers in 1903-04, whether correct or not, were, at any rate, not new to the student of economics or history. Again, it did not seem desirable to rewrite the last chapter, as would have been necessary to give a picture of the position of our industries in relation to foreign competition at the present date; for that would have involved questions of too complex a nature to have a place in a book which is mainly historical, and intended to be introductory and elementary; and, at the same time, the original slight sketch showing how the problems, which have since become more acute, appeared ten years ago, may have some permanent value. For these reasons, such alterations and additions as were necessary have been relegated to notes in an Appendix, and the main part of the book is left with its original imperfections unaltered.

A. L. B.

READING,
May, 1905.

CONTENTS

V.—TRADE IN THE PERIOD, 1870-1892.

VI.—ENGLAND'S PRESENT POSITION.

INDEX TO DIAGRAMS.

PRINCIPAL DATES CONNECTED WITH ENGLAND'S FOREIGN TRADE.

Declaration of War with France, 1793.
Spinning Jenny in use, 1798.
Union of Great Britain and Ireland, 1800.
Cartwright's Loom in use, 1801.
Peace of Amiens, 1802.
Berlin Decrees, and Orders in Council, 1807.
War with America, 1812-15.
Waterloo, 1815.
Resumption of Cash Payments, 1819.
Petition of Merchants, 1820.
Commercial Crisis, 1825.
Settlement in West Australia, 1829.
First English Railway, 1830.
First American Railway, 1832.
East India Company's Charter repealed, 1833.
Settlement in South Australia, 1834.
Commercial Crisis, 1836.
Wheatstone's Telegraph, 1837.
First Ocean Steamer, 1838.
Commercial Crisis, 1839.
Penny Post established, 1840.
Settlement in New Zealand, 1840.
Hume's Tariff Committee, 1840.
Ceding of Hong-Kong, 1841.
Paris and Rouen Railway, 1842.
Peel's Fiscal Reforms, 1842.
" " 1845.
Irish Potato Famine, 1845.
Repeal of Corn Laws, 1846.
Gold Discovery in California, 1847.
Commerical Crisis, 1847.
Navigation Laws repealed, 1849.
International Exhibition, 1851.
First Submarine Telegraph, 1851.
Gold Discovery in Australia, 1851.

Gladstone's Fiscal Reforms, 1852.
Crimean War, 1854-56.
Bessemer's Steel Patent, 1856.
War with China, 1856.
Indian Mutiny, 1857.
Commercial Crisis, 1857.
Commercial Treaty with France, 1860.
American Civil War, 1861-65.
Reduction of Prussian Duties, 1862.
Austro-German War, 1866.
Commercial Crisis, 1866.
Suez Canal, 1869.
Franco-Prussian War, 1870-71.
Commencement of Fall of Rupee, 1872.
Demonetisation of Silver by the Latin Union, 1874.
Heavy Commercial Failures, 1875.
Russo-Turkish War, 1877-78.
German Tariff increased, 1879 and 1885.
Russian Tariff increased, 1881, 1882, 1884-5, and 1890.
Austro-Hungarian Tariff increased, 1882.
Transvaal Gold Discoveries, 1885.
Great Trade Depression, 1886.
Sherman Silver Act, 1890.
McKinley Tariff, 1890.
Commercial Crisis, 1890.
Reduction of many European Tariffs, but increase of French, 1891-2.
Australian and American Bank Failures, 1893.
Sherman Act repealed, 1893.
Indian Mint closed to Silver, 1893.
Wilson Tariff, reducing U.S.A. Duties, 1894.
Dingley Tariff, increasing U.S.A. Duties, 1897.
Canada's Preferential Tariff, 1898.
South African War, 1899-1902.
Commonwealth of Australia inaugurated, 1901.
Sugar Duty imposed in United Kingdom, 1901.
Brussels Sugar Convention, 1902.
Corn Duty in United Kingdom, 1902-3.
Cape Colony's Preferential Tariff, 1903.

[For more detail, see Board of Trade Memorandum, Ed. 1761, pp. 5-9.]

ENGLAND'S FOREIGN TRADE IN THE NINETEENTH CENTURY

I.—INTRODUCTORY.

1. ENGLAND'S COMMERCIAL CONDITION INTERNALLY.

THE history of foreign trade is inextricably bound up with the general history of the development of civilisation in the nineteenth century; without foreign trade this development could not have taken place, while progress in all directions has in turn reacted on the growth of trade.

The beginning of this progress in knowledge, power and intercourse may be traced back to the inventions of the spinning-jenny, the steam-engine, and other mechanical appliances, which took place in the latter half of the eighteenth century. These inventions produced manufactures; manufactures needed and found purchasers, not only at home, but in the colonies, America, and the Continent; increased and profitable exchange gave renewed stimulus to science, which continually gave birth to new inventions, not only in manufacture, but in every branch of human labour; machinery superseded hand-labour, the quantity produced by the same amount of work, differently applied, was indefinitely increased; labour was spared from agriculture, and used in the manufactures and arts, placing within everyone's reach things hitherto costly or unknown, and adding to the comfort and luxury of common life in a way which we, who regard the cheap possession of the most finished products of the most complicated machinery as a matter of course, cannot well realise.

Meanwhile manufacture at home was found so profitable that England ceased to provide her own food, but in new and distant countries hardy pioneers were content to send us the fruit of virgin soil in return for the products of our machinery; both the new and old countries were enriched by this exchange, and both our colonies and the half-cultivated tracts of older States were populated and rendered prosperous. At home population was congregating into cities, and the stimulating effect of busy city life was hastening the process of the application of the forces of nature to the performance of the hard work formerly done by man, and of the consequent increase of labour needing brain-power rather than physical strength.

But these changes were not made easily, old customs, old ideas, old virtues almost, had to be rooted out and new ones planted, prejudices stood in the way. Trade was not free, many of its natural outlets were absolutely blocked in every country, and while it was not understood what benefits would accrue from freedom, classes interested in old established industries understood very well what injury might come to themselves. The development was thus hindered for half a century, till it had gathered force to overcome all resistance.

With the freedom of trade came an expansion of statistical and economic knowledge, and the relative powers, populations, and resources of the nations of the world gradually became matters of common knowledge.

Thus this development of foreign trade was essential both to our manufactures and to the general furtherance of what for want of a more exact name is called civilisation.

It is convenient to divide the economic results of inventions into two classes—the increase of efficiency, which would be discussed in a history of home trade, and the division of labour, which concerns us now.

Foreign trade is merely the carrying out of the principle of the division of labour. The benefits of this division are even more obvious when we are dealing with countries with different products, different climates, and different aptitudes and habits of work, than when dealing with people of the same habits in the same country.

During the years 1790-1870 the history of foreign trade is the history of the division of the world into new countries producing raw materials and old countries manufacturing them. That this is so may be seen by considering the period 1870-1873, the climax of this century's commerce, when the inflation and following depression were mainly due to a too great acceleration of this process of division, when new countries produced more raw materials than old countries could profitably manufacture.

This division was in its nature only temporary, for each new country, as it grew and prospered, has taken to manufacturing, and at present no broad distinction can be made; trade is still so hampered by artificial hindrances that the natural divisions cannot show themselves, but it seems probable that, with the varied resources and aptitudes that all countries possess in themselves, a very complex and intricate sub-division of work throughout the world will ultimately be established.

It was obviously impossible to import raw materials and export manufactures, to make the world one great workshop, each part in intimate connection with all the others, without a development of transport and communication undreamt of in the eighteenth century. But the genius of invention has proved equal to all calls on his resources; having first given the impetus, he was prepared to find the means; canals, railways, steamers, electricity were ready directly they were wanted, and no doubt new needs will find equally quick satisfaction.

We can sum up in three words—inventions, foreign trade, division of labour.

Let us now glance at the state of England at the end of the eighteenth century, bearing in mind that the changes from that to her present condition would have been impossible without foreign trade. There were very limited manufactures, in our present sense of the word, no ships to carry our superfluous goods, no foreign demand for them, no admission to other countries: the products of machinery were known to our ancestors of four generations ago as little as to savage races now.

The population of Great Britain and Ireland was 16,000,000 in 1801; in 1901 it was 41,500,000. Total imports and exports were £37,000,000 in 1791; in 1901 they were £870,000,000. At the same time, the average income and capital has increased greatly.

In fact, in the eighteenth century foreign trade was of so little importance to the majority of the inhabitants of England, that, but for some importation of wheat, the whole might have been destroyed without making any appreciable change in the habits or wealth of the people; the rich would have been deprived of some luxuries, the poor of very few, a small class of traders would have been affected, and an unimportant branch of revenue destroyed; but no other result would have followed.

This was shown by the little change which the great difficulties in the way of trade at the end of the century, during the wars with France, made in our habits, apart from the distress caused by the restriction of the wheat supply.

It will be our object to trace briefly the causes and events which have led to this startling development.

The invention and improvement of machinery, which made it profitable to manufacture in England goods which were in excess of our home consumption and became in demand elsewhere, specialised our industry, increased its output, gave employment to our growing population, and facilitated transport; and that exchange of manufactures for food, which is the backbone of our trade, was necessarily initiated.

Till the nineteenth century we were an agricultural nation, even exporting corn to the Continent. A large class of yeomen, now hardly in existence, had from time immemorial tilled their own land, and subsisted almost entirely on its produce. Every village had its common-field, where the peasants added to their wages by rights of pasture and cultivation, needing few things that could not be obtained at home or at the nearest market-town.

At a few towns special crafts flourished, but for the most part those manufactures, which now condense the population so markedly in our great towns, if they were in existence at all, were carried on in scattered villages; and the only function of the town was to be the market, the headquarters of the sale, while annual country fairs were the occasion of an important part of the countryfolk's purchases.

London was at once the general market of the kingdom, the seat of many localised trades (tailors, silversmiths, etc.), and, with Bristol and Glasgow, the emporium of all foreign goods, which thence filtered very slowly through the country.

Many of the main roads were all but impassable, for the improvement of the great coach roads took place at a later date, and only reached its climax just before they were rendered comparatively superfluous by railways; travelling was the privilege of the rich, and migration of labour was almost unknown.

One of the effects of this difficulty of transport was to make trade in articles of large bulk and small value out of the question when any substitute whatever could be obtained close at hand. For instance, no one would use coal where wood was to be had; the iron foundries were established in the neighbourhood of forests that wood might be at hand for smelting; nothing would be of iron that could be made of wood; and while in Cornwall even small houses would be built of granite, in other counties granite would only be used for the most costly buildings.

Goods can now be brought from the most distant countries at less risk, less expense, and in almost the same time, as they could then be transported from London to the extreme parts of England.

The necessity of obtaining wheat from abroad had overcome the expenses of importation more than once in bad seasons before the end of last century. Indeed, there is no country which, if dependent on its own resources, is not in perennial danger of famine; even now, whole provinces of China, Russia, or India may be devastated by a bad harvest. Before 1790 the only foreign goods we imported on a large scale were silk, hemp, wine and tropical produce.

Till the growth of the cotton trade, which may be perhaps considered to date from 1750, woollen cloth was our only export of importance. Since the time of Edward III., the Government had taken great care to foster the trade. Till the beginning of the nineteenth century, English cloth was entirely made of home-grown wool, and that there might be a plentiful supply, exportation of wool or sheep was forbidden under heavy penalties. The wool was all home-spun in cottages, villages, or towns, and either carried to market by the spinner (as flax was till recently carried in Ireland), or collected by travelling merchants for manufacture.

Even of this, which formed our one export trade, by far the larger portion was used at home. The era of trade with other countries had not arrived: our relations with them were chiefly political, and our rulers more frequently concerned with international war than with international trade.

2. ENGLAND'S COMMERCIAL RELATIONS ABROAD.

Till after the Napoleonic War the most important part of our foreign trade was with our colonies. "Settlements," or "plantations," as they used to be called, were apparently regarded by the home Government as under a favour in being allowed the use of the land on which they had settled; and, in consequence, every restriction might rightly, it was considered, be imposed to prevent their benefiting themselves in any way which could possibly have injurious effects on England or English trade.

They were therefore obliged to export all their produce to us, and only through us to other countries; they were not allowed to undertake any manufactures themselves nor to purchase manufactures from any but the mother country, and no trade whatever might be carried on except in English ships. The relations of all other European countries with their colonies were on the same plan. The American War of Independence in reality gave this system its death-blow, but it continued in force till the era of Free Trade; and the French War actually benefited the West Indian colonies, for, when the commercial restrictions of Napoleon and England were generally being set at defiance, colonial produce was exported in American ships direct to the Continent.

The "plantations" were essentially dependent on exporting their produce, and by virtue of the above regulations were obliged to purchase clothes and manufactures from us. Hence a trade, by no means contemptible, existed between England and the Indies, East and West; tropical produce came to England, and our growing manufactures had for some time a sufficient outlet. It was when the supply exceeded the wants both of the nation at home and the colonies, that the pressing need for continental trade was felt. Our imports from the East and West Indies were 50% of our total imports in 1785, but only about 8% in 1903.

A further effect was to make England an emporium for tropical produce and Oriental goods; all trade with the East was obliged to pass round the Cape, and London was, therefore, a not inconvenient centre of distribution.

England was the victor in the European competition for colonial expansion which marked the eighteenth century. The Spanish, Dutch, and French were all obliged to give way to England, and the mass of trade with the East was under English control. The East Indian, as other smaller colonial trades, was in the hands of a company which monopolised commerce with all countries east of Persia; which ruled kingdoms and carried on wars on its own account; brought to England for distribution through Europe the treasures, silks, fruits, spices, and jewels of India; and in its own immediate interest made scarce and dear goods that have since, owing to competition and improved transport, become plentiful and cheap.

Ireland was regarded in much the same light as the colonies: no concession was allowed to her which could be supposed to injure England. Manufacture of glass and the drapery trade were suppressed, and her agriculture injured by bounties on corn exports from England. She was injured both by the restrictions forced on her and by the unwise privileges, such as the bounties on exportation of corn and manufactures, which the Irish Parliament of 1784 granted to special trades.[1]

The trade between England and the United States of America has always been of the greatest importance both to us and to them. It was greatly unsettled by the War of Independence (1776); but the absolute necessity to the States of having England as an outlet for her cotton, and the growing advantage of the cotton trade to both countries, tended to establish commerce on a sound and permanent basis.

Our European trade, owing to the perpetual wars

[1] For a full discussion of this subject, see Cunningham's "Growth of English Industry and Commerce," vol. ii., pp. 523-529 (1st Edition); or in 1903 Edition "Modern Times," pp. 372-6,521-2,546.

with France, was subject to great vicissitudes from the earliest times till long after the Napoleonic War; but the genius for trading of the Dutch had, except during the short periods that we were openly at war with them, kept open a means of communication with Central Europe, and our trade with the States bordering on the Baltic was regular and sound, if undeveloped.

All the commercial relations between country and country were marred by what may be called international prejudice. Every admission of imports from abroad was regarded as a concession at the expense of the importing nation, only to be made when necessary to obtain a similar concession, or when forced by a stronger power. Trade was not regarded as beneficial to the purchaser, but only as profitable to the vendor. This, at least, was the politician's and popular view, and merchants were only beginning to realise the fallacy of it.

3. DIVISION OF LABOUR.

All exchange is a sign of division of labour, and is an advantage to both parties concerned, for otherwise the exchange would not be made. This has always been recognised in transactions between fellow-countrymen; but, when members of two nations are concerned, other considerations, based fundamentally on political or social disadvantages, supposed to follow changes in the course of a nation's trade, and also on a want of imagination in realising the actual transactions, have often hidden the possibility of using a foreign neighbour's special opportunities and skill to save native work.

Of all the phenomena of human development, it is perhaps no exaggeration to say that the progress of division of labour has been the most continuous and the most gradual. It requires and makes use of every improvement in skill, every means of more rapid and intimate communication, every advance in mutual confidence, in security, and in freedom; and in each of these there is still prospect of unlimited progress.

It is worth while to trace lightly this development in England since the Middle Ages.

In feudal times, within the precincts of each castle, many trades were carried on; the insecurity of life and property preventing industries elsewhere. Here we have labour, divided indeed, but only among some few score hands.

But even in so small a country as England different localities have necessarily different products. Copper and tin must come from Wales or Cornwall, or not at all. The highlands will not produce the corn and pasture of the lowlands. Hence trade arose between the mines and the rest of the country; and that form of division, where one man works and another takes the produce by force, doing his share if at all by fighting a common enemy, was also prevalent. Again, certain men have certain natural faculties; the Jew had a faculty for accumulating, and this was used by the less provident baron.

In the course of time trades became specialised to certain towns, both by the increase of prosperity and wealth of special crafts in them, and especially by the settlement of bodies of foreign weavers or spinners, as at Spitalfields and Norwich. And gradually, as opportunity allowed, it was recognised that East Anglia was specially productive of wheat, Kent the suitable district for hops, the Cotswold Hills and Salisbury Plain the natural home of the shepherd, while potteries were most successful in the midlands.

From Saxon times we hear of commerce with the Continent, whenever a powerful and peaceful king encouraged it; the Crusades gave England some knowledge of the fabled wealth of the East, and Indian shawls and jewels came overland along the prehistoric caravan routes to Europe, and so to England. Thus acquaintance was made with goods that could by no possibility be produced in England, and the foundation of division of labour among nations was laid.

But our immediate neighbours, when we were not at war with them, had wines and silks to sell us which could not be rivalled here; and trade naturally stepped across the Channel.

With the colonisation of America, England's productive resources were extended; Englishmen could now grow sugar and tobacco, and it was never thought that full trade between them and the mother country was not legitimate, so long as they offered us nothing that we could produce ourselves.

The fact still to be understood was that it was profitable to obtain from abroad produce which we were already growing for ourselves; that though, for instance, two nations have rich mines, a little difference in the difficulties of working them may make it worth while for one to leave its minerals untouched, and grow corn to exchange for the ores of the other.

Prices, which in the long run are the true index of the direction in which labour can most economically be applied, showed many channels of exchange long before governments allowed exports and imports. And it was exactly this question which was fought out in the campaign which terminated in the repeal of the Corn Laws in 1846.

Once allowed free play, labour very speedily became divided between countries, each producing for the other the wealth for which it was most suited.

One or two instances may be given of the marvellous extent to which this division is carried out.

Italy can grow both Indian corn and cotton; but America supplies her with corn, and India with cotton.

Till recently cotton was exported in vast quantities from India and America to England, to be there manufactured, exported, and sold again in the lands where it was grown.

The element strontium is obtained in Argyle, and sent immense distances to sugar refineries, to effect a trifling chemical economy in crystallisation.

Malta obtains soil from Sicily and roots from England, and carries on an export trade in potatoes.

In the process of obtaining finished leather, skins cross the ocean four times to effect economies in subordinate treatments.

In 1800, some specialisation was already in existence besides that which different climates made inevitable. England was the home of woollen and cotton manufactures, America and parts of Europe exported surplus corn, timber came from Scandinavia, hemp from Russia, metals from Spain, and wines from the most famous vintages. But little progress had been made; even internal trade was not free.

That immense economies even now remain to be effected there can be no doubt. If the principle that each nation should produce only that for which it is most suited were carried out, our foreign might equal our home trade, and that of all nations be brought up to the same level; but there are many causes which prevent the rapid division of industries among countries, and there is a definite limit which can be reached.

In the process of division much must be sacrificed. Town after town, county after county has lost its trade, owing to a cheaper and better production of its staple produce elsewhere. Little loss has fallen to the country as a whole, because other industries have necessarily been developed, but the result is, of course, a migration of population.

Similarly, a nation may lose its greatest branch of trade, and obtain no other; and the flow of population will take place in exactly the same way as from town to town, or (to take an historical case) from the south to the north of England; many countries have thus fallen in power and population. It may thus be a true instinct which foresees the decadence of national prosperity in any special change of industry. If permanently lower prices will follow the change, it must be profitable, but a trade which depends on foreign custom is always liable to be displaced; steps forward in this development cannot be retraced, and the inevitable result will be that one country will be sacrificed for the economic benefit of the world. This sacrifice may often be a greater price than the world, or the country, would willingly pay.

The limit to the indefinite division is to be found in the social, intellectual, and moral objections to specialisation. It is not pleasant to contemplate England as one vast factory, an enlarged Manchester, manufacturing in semi-darkness, continual uproar, and at intense pressure for the rest of the world. Nor would the continent of America, divided into square, numbered fields, and cultivated from a central station by electricity, be an ennobling spectacle. Variety will be essential till the æsthetic side of man is destroyed.

The division of intellectual labour is exactly analogous, and has proceeded step by step in the same way.

In the time of Roger Bacon, a philosopher was acquainted with all the learning of which the world was then in possession. Four centuries later, Newton was known as a mathematician, and not celebrated as metaphysician or theologian. In this century, division has continued with enormous acceleration.

Knowledge of languages has branched till etymology and ethnology each require a lifetime's study. At Cambridge there are six professors of entirely distinct branches of mathematics. In natural history one man will devote his whole energy to a small group of one species; in fact, instances could be given and multiplied. Moreover, the evils as well as the benefits of specialisation are as obvious and as prevalent as in the commercial world.

4. DIGRESSION ON CHANGES IN THE VALUE OF GOLD AND THE USE OF INDEX NUMBERS.

No comparison of any value can be made between prices and wages current at times separated by a long interval, unless we have some means of comparing the value of money at the two dates.

The slightest consideration shows this when we are trying to realise the meaning of any statements of expenditure in the Middle Ages: for instance, when we read that "threepence yearly for each house in the High Street of Leicester that had a gable" was a sufficient bribe to buy important concessions from the Earl of Leicester,[1] we know that we are reading about coins whose value has no relation to the pence we use, though they may be of a similar mould; but when we open a statistical abstract and see

	1877.	1891.
Wheat . .	13s.	9s. 5d.

we are inclined to think that, in dealing with dates within our own memory, money has the same value, and a shilling means the same thing in 1877 and 1891. But, as a matter of fact, in 1891 1s. would go as far in ordinary purchases as 1s. 3d. in 1877, and neglect of this fact will give us quite erroneous ideas about the fall in the price of wheat. We might, perhaps, without this caution, prove to our satisfaction that English

[1] Green's "Short History of the English People," p. 189.

agriculture must be hopelessly ruined by such a fall in price, while full allowance for the change in the purchasing power of money would give quite a different impression.

It is partly owing to neglect of the fact that this purchasing power has increased continuously since 1873, that the continual cries of commercial depression obtain such ready credence.

Till we have obtained a method of comparing the actual values of money at different dates, we are not in a position to make any statement, except the vaguest, about prices and trade at different dates.

The object of this section is to explain the method by which this has been done.

The effects of foreign trade are twofold: it brings within our reach goods which otherwise we could not obtain, and it offers us articles with which we are already familiar at a reduced price. In order to measure this second effect, it is necessary to compare prices at different dates.

Prices must therefore be brought to some standard. Naturally they are reckoned in gold, but the price of gold changes just in the same way as that of everything else, the advantage of its use as a standard of value being that its changes are generally gradual, and only perceptible after a long interval. But any cause which makes gold more plentiful or more easy to obtain lowers its value; more gold must be given for other products, and prices rise.

A more constant standard must therefore be obtained by which we can trace, and then allow for, the variations of gold. This has been accomplished in the following way:—An imaginary budget is made out of a great variety of goods, wheat, cotton, wool, manufactures, tea, sugar, and so on; a definite quantity of each is taken in proportion to its importance; this budget is then valued at the prices current for each article for each different year. One date is taken as a standard, say when the budget comes to £100. If in any year the budget comes to less than £100, less gold will buy the same goods, prices generally have fallen, gold is scarce: if it be greater than £100, more gold is required for the same goods, prices have risen, gold is plentiful.

The year that will generally be taken in this essay is 1871. The imaginary budget being worked out and priced in that year as 100, corresponding numbers (index numbers) have been found for each year by Sauerbeck. Then any price in any year can be valued in gold as in 1871 by simple proportion. For instance, the number for 1889 is 72. £72 would go as far in 1889 as £100 in 1871. An article that cost £72 in 1889 would cost £100 with gold at the value of 1871. Therefore to find the price of any article in 1889, at the gold value of 1871, the current price must be multiplied by $\frac{100}{72}$.

Put in a different way, we find by this method what quantity of these staple articles must be given in return for any other article whatever. Thus coffee was £3 5s. per cwt. in 1886, £3 3s. in 1871. That is, at the earlier date less gold was given in return for coffee than at the later. But in 1886, prices generally were low, and the index number is 67. $\frac{100}{67}$ of £3 5s. is £4 17s., and this is the amount to be compared with

1871. Hence we see that in 1886, the price of coffee measured in other staple articles had risen 50 per cent.

The prices of wheat in 1871 and 1886 were 11s. 10d. and 7s. 6d. respectively. $\frac{100}{67}$ of 7s. 6d. is 11s. 2d. Hence wheat had actually, as well as apparently, fallen in value during that period, when compared with other produce.

A remarkable proof of the accuracy of index numbers is obtained by examining the shipping statistics, as will be seen later;[1] for on drawing the two curves representing the one, the tons of shipping entered and cleared at our ports, the other, total imports and exports valued at 1871 prices, it is almost impossible to separate them. These numbers, though necessarily founded on partial information, bear a close relation to the actual facts.

Index numbers give no clue to the amount of labour expended in producing a given quantity of goods; that must be decided by other considerations. But we find by them exactly when one article became cheap relatively to others; and if, for instance, we find that certain foreign produce was at a lower price (relatively) after a change of tariff, we can say that the reduction was not due to any fluctuation of money values, but (in the absence of other causes) to the change of tariff. We have a means of finding the relative changes in price that followed any cause whose effects we wish to investigate.

The index number has also two more important uses. In the first place, we can find the changes in the *quantity* of imports or exports when we have

[1] *Vide* V. 4 *infra*.

only data of the changes in money *value.* For, in the mass, goods imported and exported are just those whose changes we have allowed for in forming the index number. By this means we shall find that the quantity (weight or volume) of imports and exports has shown a very steady and constant growth, at dates when the money values show considerable fluctuations; and we shall find that commercial depressions are often only depressions in price, while the volume of trade continues as great as ever.

In the second place, we can compare wages[1] at different periods. If a man's wages were 25s. in 1871, and 30s. in 1886, an increase of 20 per cent., this represents only a small part of the actual increase; for in 1886 (index number 67), 67s. would buy what cost 100s. in 1871. Hence 30s. will buy in 1886 what would cost ($\frac{100}{67}$ of 30s. =) 45s. in 1871; the increase in the amount which the man can purchase is 80 per cent. Without making this allowance, comparison of wages is impracticable.

A reduction of prices may be brought about in three ways. First, by a scarcity of gold; and this cause can be to a great extent eliminated by using the index number. Secondly, an increased efficiency in production owing to machinery, or better use of natural resources, gives more produce in return for the same labour, and, if there is not a corresponding increase in the currency, we shall definitely "get more for our money." Thirdly, a new trade with a foreign country will enable us to pay for goods from

[1] *Vide* pp. 105-6 *infra*. Special index numbers must be formed for wage comparisons.

abroad with manufactures which we can easily make, and which our foreign customers desire. For instance, when we began to buy foreign corn with manufactured goods, we obtained it at a much lower price than we had paid for corn grown on bad soil at home.[1] A redistribution of trade among countries and nations may have a great effect in lowering prices. The changes due to this source are often comparatively easily traced, and it is with these changes that we are chiefly concerned in connection with foreign trade.

The prices which changes in foreign trade may be expected to affect are, first, the prices of those goods which are imported (an improvement in the sources of trade being shown by a reduced price), and secondly, of the goods exported in return; for an enlarged market has in many cases the effect of making all those economies which are due to manufacturing on a large scale possible, and competition in foreign markets gives the stimulus for improved methods and new inventions. Cotton goods would not now be so cheap in England if our factories had never produced them except for home consumption.

[1] Before the repeal of the Corn Laws, the necessity for increased supplies of corn was so great that the worst as well as the best ground was ploughed, and it was, of course, the work necessary on the inferior land that governed the prices.

II.—THE FRENCH WARS, 1793-1815.

1. THE EXPENSE OF THE WAR AND HINDRANCES TO TRADE.

THE year 1793 is the natural date at which to begin a review of the nineteenth century's trade, because just before that date prices and trade were in a condition typical of the eighteenth century, and because that was the date of the commencement of the war that ushered in the present century, and which had such important effects in stamping permanent characteristics on the foreign trade of this and other countries.

Briefly, the history of the war is as follows:—In consequence of the attitude of the French after the Revolution, war was declared between England and France in 1793. The injuries inflicted on the trade and vessels of neutral nations led to the formation of a coalition of Russia, Sweden, and Denmark in an armed neutrality; this led to the battle of Copenhagen, and the coalition was dissolved. Hostilities were suspended for a year in 1802, and on the renewal of the war Russia joined Austria and England. The French were beaten at sea in the battle of Trafalgar in 1805, but by land Austria and Russia were in the same year defeated at Austerlitz. The next stage in the war was Wellington's campaign in Spain,

1807-1814, which he gradually conquered, and whence he marched on France. Meanwhile Napoleon undertook a disastrous expedition into Russia, from which he retreated with great loss (1812), and in 1814 France was attacked on all sides, and Napoleon abdicated and retired to Elba.

He returned in 1815, and a very rapid campaign culminated in the battle of Waterloo, in which the French were totally defeated, and Napoleon was imprisoned in St. Helena.

From 1812 to 1815 we were also engaged in a war with the United States of America, owing to the injurious effects of our policy on neutral trade.

In times of peace during the eighteenth century, England's normal public expenditure was less than £15,000,000 per annum ; during the twenty-two years of war the average was £69,000,000, so that the expense of the war may be estimated in round numbers as £1,000,000,000. This was the amount which was withdrawn from productive labour. With this pecuniary expense there was a constant drain of able-bodied men from all employments. In thousands of families the bread-winner was at the war, and absolute poverty was in many houses, while labourers could hardly be obtained for necessary work.

The distress was increased by a succession of some of the worst harvests on record, in 1794, 1795, 1799, 1800, 1804, 1809.

From 1793-1804, prices were far above the former average, owing to the badness of these seasons, the expense or impossibility of importation, and the high rate of interest, which was caused by the immense loans to the Government. Wages of agricultural labourers and artisans necessarily rose, or they could not have obtained a bare subsistence; while such was the disorganisation of manufacturing trades, that factory hands did not obtain an adequate increase, and were on the brink of starvation.

For many years the whole nation was kept at high tension, owing to the immediate expectation of an invasion of the French, for which preparations were being made within sight of our coasts, and by an exaggerated fear of Napoleon, who was regarded as possessing almost supernatural powers. Every nerve was strained to procure money, ships, and men for the struggle, and the interests of trade were not only directly injured, but suffered also from neglect.

During these years our foreign trade was often reduced almost to *nil*. The peculiarity of this war was that strenuous attacks were directed against the trade of the enemy as well as against the hostile forces. Ships, sailing under neutral flags, were overhauled, and confiscated if containing goods for the enemy; and colonial trade was a special object of attack. The dangers of transport were so great that the rate for insurance was prohibitory. In 1808 the price of 80s. per quarter for wheat produced no importation; in 1810 freight, insurance, and licence amounted to 50s. per quarter. The contest of this nature was at its height when orders in council were issued in England, 1807, decreeing that "no vessel shall be permitted to trade from one port to another, both which ports shall belong to or be in the possession of France or her allies, or shall be so far under their control as that British vessels may not freely trade thereat"; and further, that "all such ports shall be considered in a state of blockade"; which Napoleon answered in the Berlin and Milan decrees, declaring the British Isles in a state of blockade, prohibiting all correspondence with them, and declaring all Englishmen abroad prisoners of war, all English goods confiscate, and forbidding any nation whatsoever to obey the "orders in council." As a consequence, quantities of English goods were burnt in Hamburg and elsewhere.

Thus the effects of the war were first to give a stimulus to our trade with Russia and other countries which supplied us with naval or military stores; then to stop our trade with France and the countries of the armed neutrality till 1800; while after the peace of Amiens, the ports of Russia and the Baltic countries were open, but the risks of transport were almost prohibitory, and trade with the rest of Europe, which was under French influence, was stopped as far as it was possible for arbitrary enactments to hinder it. Finally, American trade was hopelessly disorganised from 1812 to 1815. In spite of all these obstacles, not only was progress made internally, but our export trade actually increased; while £22,000,000 was the highest value of exports before 1793, the average from 1805-1815 was £41,000,000.

Arkwright's inventions had been released from patent rights in 1798; Cartwright's loom had come into use in 1801; woollen, cotton, and silk industries were growing, and there was great demand for both goods and machines on the Continent. The efforts

DIAGRAM II.

Showing fluctuations of Imports and Exports during the War

A EXPORTS. B IMPORTS

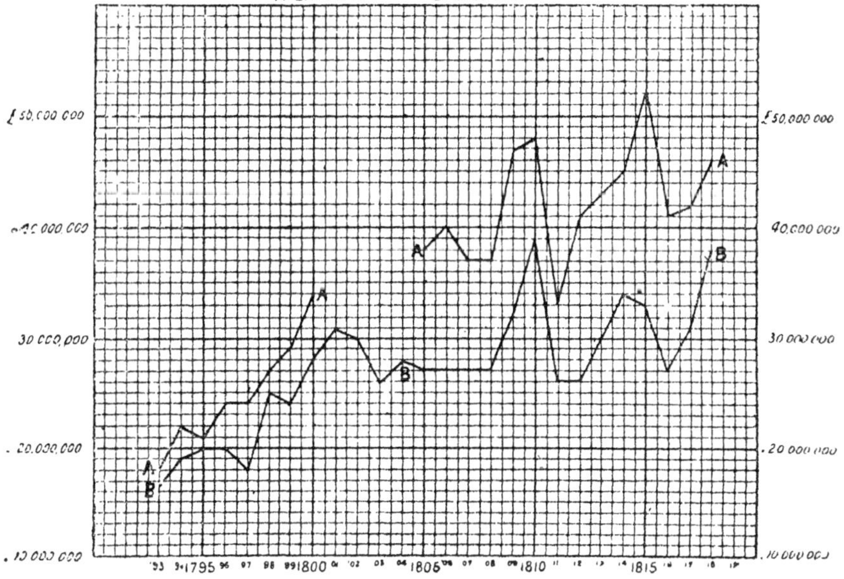

No Figures obtainable for Exports 1800-05

made to evade the Milan and Berlin decrees were so great that a fall in prices and a commercial crisis followed in 1811, because in hope of the great prices to be obtained on the Continent more goods had passed the barriers than could find a market which paid for so great expense. Trade, driven from straightforward methods, adopted every devious means of eluding the prohibitory decrees. Ships sailed under false colours, and with false papers, and changed their destination when on voyage. Goods were landed at night, or took most circuitous routes to reach their market. A spirit of gambling and speculation induced the boldest hazards, and many romantic adventures and hair-breadth escapes were the result. At each short cessation of hostilities immense quantities of goods were shipped. "Never before was the shipping of this country employed at higher freights; and scarcely a ship belonging to any other nation could sail without a licence from the Government of this country. The whole of the exportable produce of the East and West Indies, and of a great part of South America, came to our ports; and no part of the continent of Europe could obtain a supply of coffee, sugar, and other colonial articles, or of the raw materials of some of their manufactures, except from this country."[1] For England had command of the seas, especially after the battles of the Nile, Copenhagen, and Trafalgar, and used it to her advantage.

One interesting aspect of the war is the illustration it affords of the condition of England when cut off from foreign trade.

[1] Tooke's "History of Prices," i. 105.

As regards manufactures, which were only then becoming of importance, the effect was to postpone and hinder the new developments. It is in connection with the supply of food that the period is so instructive.

The prices of corn during the years 1793-1815 were as follows:—

OFFICIAL ANNUAL AVERAGE.

	Per Quarter.		Per Quarter.		Per Quarter.
1793	49s. 3d.	1801	119s. 6d.	1809	97s. 4d.
1794	52s. 3d.	1802	69s. 10d.	1810	106s. 5d.
1795	75s. 2d.	1803	58s. 10d.	1811	95s. 3d.
1796	78s. 7d.	1804	62s. 3d.	1812	126s. 6d.
1797	53s. 9d.	1805	89s. 9d.	1813	109s. 9d.
1798	51s. 10d.	1806	79s. 1d.	1814	74s. 4d.
1799	69s. 0d.	1807	75s. 4d.	1815	75s. 7d.
1800	113s. 10d.	1808	81s. 4d.		

Since 1820 the annual average has never been above 74s. 9d.,[1] while the average from 1821-1890 is 51s. 9d. The dearth which caused these prices was exceptional in the number of successive bad harvests; but isolated seasons equally unproductive have occurred since. With the small population of nine millions[2] in 1801, wheat rose to 126s. a quarter. With the population in 1904 of thirty-four millions, a discontinuance of foreign supplies would cause a famine unequalled in the experience of Europe.

It is important to notice that the petition for cessation of the war and liberation of trade came from the Lancashire manufacturers; for the necessity for

[1] In the Crimean War.

[2] England and Wales only.

DIAGRAM III,

showing the fluctuations of annual Average Price of Wheat (per Imperial Quarter) during the War.

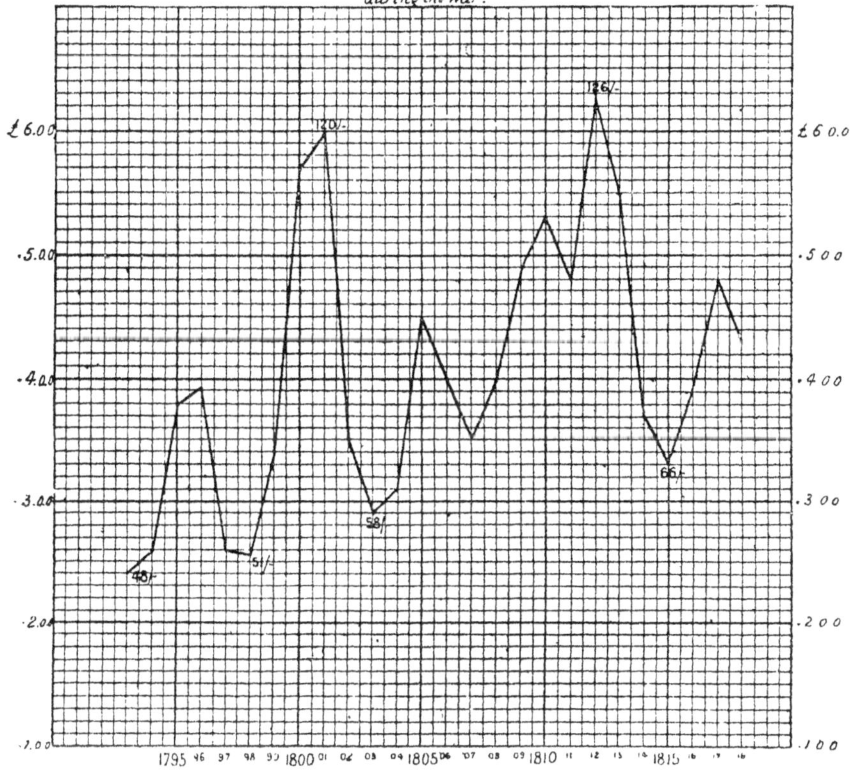

foreign trade was first felt by those who had goods to sell, not by the country in general.

The interest of the period is great at the present time in view of the long-threatened European war. Is it now possible to combine war and trade? If all Europe is fighting, and we are neutrals, shall we continue to get corn from Russia and Germany, and silk from France? Will any merchandise pass inter-European frontiers? Will there be a second Berlin decree, and will all nations, dependent as they are more than ever on supplies from each other, be thrown back on their own resources, so that each of the choicest products of civilisation, science, and commerce will have added new and terrible weapons to the armoury of nations?

2. PERMANENT EFFECTS OF THE WAR ON COMMERCE.

The victory of England in the Napoleonic War was as important in its commercial as in its political effects. In the first place, England was left in command of the seas. All her ancient rivals, at one time the Spaniards but more recently the Dutch, were beaten off the sea, and there was only left the United States of America, already suffering from the inferiority of her own wood for shipbuilding, and artificial dearness of imports. Owing to the colonial regulations, the great part of the trade of the West Indies, and practically all that of India, was ours; and no vessel, except European vessels carrying the goods of the country from which they came, could trade in our ports.[1] All this was the principle of the Navigation Law in full swing, but in that time of monopoly and protection it was esteemed a great advantage, and our supremacy at sea, being founded on real superiority, has endured.

In the second place, though the drain of money and men had been as severe in England as in the rest of Europe, yet England's credit was better, and the war had been fought in the midst of Spain, France, Germany, Russia, and Belgium, while we in our island had escaped the worst effects of its near approach.

The first of these was at once the maturing of our greatest industry, and the means of transport for the goods of others.

The second helped to give us that start in inventions, machinery, and manufactures which, though we may be naturally superior to continental nations in such ingenuity, gave us most important advantages in the race in mechanical skill which was so keen in the next generation, and enabled us to establish our reputation and throw other nations into our debt.

It was a matter of complaint that in the negotiations which followed the downfall of Napoleon, the commercial interests of England were neglected and possibilities of trade expansion, which were within our power, were allowed to lapse.

For long after the war our relations with France were seldom of an amicable nature. The French did

[1] "No subject of the King should ship any merchandise outward or homeward, save in ships of the King's allegiance, on penalty of forfeiture of vessel and cargo."

not quickly forget their defeat; every difference and dispute was exaggerated, and every disadvantage in the way of our trade considered a gain to them. Trade between near neighbours, with such different products and climates, carries benefits so obvious as to counteract this jealousy and suspicion to a limited extent; but except between the years 1860 and 1873, trade has been heavily restricted.

If, on the one hand, the Continent as a whole was so exhausted with the war that in Europe there were no longer any dangerous rivals by sea or land; on the other, the general poverty made them indifferent customers: which latter situation is more injurious to trade than the former.

Our attention is therefore turned to our colonies and to the United States of America. We were left with a free hand for colonisation, and for developing our colonial trade under the old system; and our trade with India and the East could grow peacefully. We find that the percentage of our whole exports which our colonial trade accounted for increased from 1815 to 1828, while the Indian trade grew slowly. But our condition was not altogether prosperous; our bad fiscal system, the enervating poor law, and our stupendous debt did not conduce to rapid development.

Our manufactures continuing to grow, cotton imports necessarily increased also: that is, our trade with the United States of America increased in bulk, but, owing to reduced prices, not greatly in value.

Our objectless war in 1812-15 had given an impetus to the States' mines and manufactures during the time that no imports could be obtained from us. To protect these a high tariff was imposed of 25 per cent. which, with many variations, increased to a maximum of 45 per cent. in 1830. This was the beginning of the incessant changes of and battles over the tariffs, which are now such an important factor in commercial history. It was then that many of those "interests" were created which have necessitated taxes to protect, taxes to compensate, and taxes to equalise without number. The States, like France, for long had a dislike for the English, generated at the time of the War of Independence, and amounting at critical times almost to frenzy; but it has been the policy of a party rather than universal; and we were such good customers that trade was allowed, if not promoted. The great advantages to both parties overcame natural repugnance, and trade has been the greatest source of peace between us and the Americans.

3. THE INDUSTRIAL REVOLUTION.

The change that was passing over the country during this period is generally spoken of as the Industrial Revolution.

The era of inventions began in the middle of the eighteenth century. Their tendency was twofold: first, to do by a machine every simple monotonous movement, such as combing wool, which had hitherto been accomplished by hand; secondly, to apply natural forces, water, steam, and, later, gas and electricity, to accomplish what had formerly exhausted the strength of men or animals.

The change in the meaning of the word "manufacture," originally justifying its literal meaning of "making by hand," to its present sense of producing in large quantities by the help of machinery, clearly shows the course of the woollen and cotten industries.

Woollen manufacture was naturally one of the earliest subjects of inventive skill. The motion of combing by hand was very difficult to imitate with machinery; Cartwright's first attempts failed, and till his first machines were much altered and improved, very little use could be made of them. In 1801, however, the machinery came into general use for certain classes of work.

It was entirely due to Arkwright's and Crompton's inventions of the spinning-jenny and mule that the cotton trade became of any importance. Such inventions first caused and then developed this trade, and many were afterwards modified and applied to wool spinning and cloth manufacture.

The growth of these improvements would have been of comparatively little avail without a new motive power, and concurrently with them the steam-engine was being perfected. An earlier step, however, was the use of water-power, and for a short time the neighbourhood of running streams was the chief influence in locating manufacturing districts.

Steam, which had already been used for pumping water from mines, was first applied to cotton machinery in 1785. Since then its increased application has been continuous.

In spite of the devastating effects of the war, the

population increased at a continually accelerated speed between the years 1781 and 1821. The population of England and Wales in the following years was approximately :—

1781, ...	7,400,000
1791, ...	8,200,000
1801, ...	9,200,000
1811, ...	10,800,000
1821, ...	12,700,000

In the last two decades of the eighteenth century masters and men were alike prosperous owing to the immense increase of the trade. At first the introduction of machinery employed more hands than it displaced. Every possible building was used for looms; everyone who could make a start also made a fortune; a family of workers could earn from £2 to £6 a week. Thus the increasing population was rapidly employed.

The situation led to the following state of trade :— The output soon exceeded the home, but was far below the foreign demand; raw materials were urgently needed, and, in the case of wool, with difficulty obtained. Thus imports were greatly increased, and in payment for these the manufactured articles not required at home were exported.

In the time of the war a great quantity of timber, hemp, and other stores was imported to equip the army and navy. Thus the war itself had one effect in increasing trade.

Finally, as will be immediately seen, a smaller proportion of the population was employed in agriculture ;

at the same time that the population increased, the producers of food became fewer, and the harvests failed; a great importation of wheat was necessitated, and for this again our manufactures paid.

It was under these circumstances that the struggle against the Corn Laws was generated. The new manufacturing class had no interest in keeping up the price of wheat, the special object of the landowning, which was still the most influential, class. They needed, on the other hand, cheap food for the workmen, that wages might not be unreasonably high, an open market for their goods, and foreign products in return for them.

The change in the distribution of the population is the most striking evidence of this change of the country's staple occupations.

In the first place, population was concentrated in towns. Steam effects its maximum economies when many machines can be worked by one engine, in a limited space, and where supervision and organisation are easy, so that the most profitable factories are those which employ several hundred hands in one building. Again, where trade advantages point to a district as a favourable situation, there, not one but many factories will be placed. Thus, instead of a small population engaged in weaving, spinning and combing, scattered through a large district, we have an immense crowd concentrated in one place. In 1760, there were, perhaps, twelve provincial towns of more than 10,000 inhabitants in England and Wales, of which only two (Bristol and Norwich) contained more than 50,000. In 1901, the population of 12 towns was over

200,000, of about 30 over 100,000, of about 60 over 50,000 ; but during the nineteenth century the total population of the United Kingdom had only increased three-fold.

Considered at such a wide interval, the difference may appear exaggerated ; but the process has been continuous, and its continuance is very perceptible at the present day in England, while the same proportionate growth of towns is one of the most marked features of the statistics of all industrial countries.

Secondly, the relative numbers of those engaged in agriculture and manufacture and other trades have entirely changed.

In 1760 (according to Arthur Young),
farmers (and agricultural labourers) were . . . . 33 per cent.
,, manufacturers and artisans . . . . 35 ,,
of the whole population.

In 1881, farmers (and agricultural labourers) were . . 13 per cent.
,, manufacturers . . 28 ,,
,, builders . . . . 9 ,, of the whole.

Thus agriculture has proportionately much decreased, manufacture (allowing for the different methods in which the tables were compiled) remained about the same, and other occupations increased greatly.

Thirdly, there has been a great shifting of the relative strength of the population from the south to the north.

In 1760, the counties which were most densely

peopled were Gloucester, Wilts, Somerset, Yorkshire, Norfolk, owing to the wool trade; Surrey, Herts, Bucks and Berks, from the goodness of their agriculture; and Worcester, Stafford and Northampton, from the manufactories there situated.

In 1881, London had expanded across the boundaries of Surrey and Kent; Lancashire, Durham, Stafford, Warwick, and the West Riding were the most thickly populated counties; and of the twenty-three largest provincial towns, eighteen were north of a line drawn from the Severn to the Humber. The effect of the movements of the population has, therefore, been to empty the counties in the south and in the Thames basin, to leave the midlands populous, and to increase very greatly the population of the northern counties.

This change emphasises what is meant by the "industrial revolution." We used to be an agricultural nation, self-contained and self-supporting. We became a manufacturing nation, for a long time the world's manufacturers, and till recently our exports far exceeded those of any other country. Our trade is especially to work up raw materials; our imports must, therefore, be immense to supply our factories; and since the proportion of those who produce food directly is low, we must also import wheat in great quantities.

We of this generation, born after the great battle of Free Trade was fought and won in England, can hardly realise how modern is every condition of our present trade; that barely four generations ago factories were almost unknown; and that it is only a century since our manufacturers were struggling for a hardly recognised existence, unrepresented in Parliament, with every fiscal law against them, while a great war was draining the strength of the nation, and hindering every development of commerce.

III.—THE BATTLE OVER FREE TRADE.

1. INTRODUCTORY.

IN considering a diagram[1] of English imports and exports since 1800, the first glance shows the immense increase of our foreign trade, and however familiar the fact may be, it is difficult to realise that our trade now is at least twelve times greater in pounds sterling (or allowing for the great increase in the purchasing power of money, twenty-four times greater) than it was a century ago.

On closer inspection, it is seen that the growth is naturally divided into four periods: from 1800 to 1826, when trade is almost stagnant; from 1826 to 1846, when imports increased at the continued rate of $3\frac{1}{2}$ per cent. per annum;[2] from 1846 to 1872, when trade progressed at an enormous rate, imports increasing nearly four-fold in twenty-six years, or at the rate of $6\frac{1}{10}$ per cent. per annum;[3] and from 1872 onwards, a period which is not yet complete, and which is characterised by three great fluctuations, with the result that imports had increased about 50 per cent. by 1903 (population having increased about 33

[1] *Vide* Diagram i.

[2] £38,000,000 (Imports in 1826) $\times \left(\frac{103.5}{100}\right)^{20}$ = £76,000,000 (Imports in 1846).

[3] £76,000,000 $\times \left(\frac{106.1}{100}\right)^{26}$ = £355,000,000 (Imports in 1872).

per cent.), while the proportion of total imports and exports to population was nearly the same in 1872 and 1903.

Considering next in rough outline the historical events which we should expect to affect our trade, we find that effects follow causes very closely.

The effects of the war which we have already considered, and the exhaustion which followed it, fully account for the character of the diagram in the first period.

The peace which continued without interruption for forty years is shown with equal clearness in the progress of trade.

In 1820, the battle of Free Trade was begun by the "Petition of the Merchants," and with sometimes slow, sometimes rapid success, was fought till 1846, the date of the repeal of the Corn Laws. During this time English history deals almost entirely with home politics. This is our second period, which it is hard to separate from the third, the great period of expansion. For the new stream of science and invention which rose in the middle of the eighteenth century was diverted by war, restricted by monopolies, and dammed by the artificial barriers of tariffs and customs; but when these hindrances were removed, the risen flood burst all bounds, and carried our commerce to a mark which the ordinary current of trade has only recently enabled us to pass.

With the acceptance of Free Trade, business expanded with immense rapidity: the extension of railways, the introduction of steam ships, the use of the telegraph, the discovery of gold in Australia and

California, the growing importance of the colonies, and the opening of the Suez Canal, combined with the increasing liberality of foreign tariffs to continually supply new impetus.

In 1871 Europe was disturbed politically by the Franco-Prussian War, and in 1873 commercially by the payment to Germany of the war-indemnity of £20,000,000; this marked the end of the expansion.

It is worth notice that every event of importance during the century is reflected on the trade diagrams, just as every political disturbance is reflected at once on the bourses; and, conversely, to each sudden change corresponds an event. For instance, the most marked depressions in the total imports and exports line up to 1873 are in 1805, 1811, 1861, and 1866, the dates of the battle of Trafalgar, American War, American Civil War, and Austro-German War, and in detailed[1] figures of trade with each country the chief events are equally marked.

It is proposed to deal with the periods before 1850, 1850-1870, and since 1870, separately, in this and the following chapters.

2. PRINCIPLES AND HISTORY OF FREE TRADE.

[See Note 1, p. 148.]

No sketch of our commerce would be complete without at least a short account of the principles and historical applications of Free Trade.

The principles which the words "Free Trade" cover are, very briefly, as follows:—

[1] *Vide* Diagrams viii. and x.

1. The advantage of trade is mutual: in selling, each party obtains something which he prefers to his own goods, and which he cannot make easily for himself.

2. Exactly the same applies when traders are of different countries, under all circumstances, except that transport is more expensive, the risk of conveyance is greater, and trade is less stable, being liable to disturbance by war and political events.

3. When goods can be obtained at a cheaper rate in one market than another, it generally signifies that that species of work can be done more efficiently or with less labour in the former locality; buying in that market, in preference to others, is, therefore, a means of furthering a division of labour, in which every district is engaged in the work which is most suited to it.

4. The disadvantages, loss and suffering, which attend every development of trade that implies change of occupation or situation, come in just the same way whether the whole change is accomplished in one country or involves several. In each case the temporary misfortune of the few is the price of the permanent advantage of the many.

5. It is not possible to obtain imports unless we have exports with which to pay for them. Therefore, the internal trade of a country can only be altered, not diminished, by an increase of foreign trade. Further, the more imports appear to be crowding out home goods, the greater our exports, or the greater the price paid for the same quantity.

6. Governments cannot increase trade; their efforts

to direct it have generally been injurious; the only active course they can take is to erect barriers between countries, which have exactly the same evil effects that barriers between counties or towns in the same kingdom would have.

Though the principles and logic of Free Trade have never been logically refuted, it is regarded as at best an impracticable theory by the majority of nations, and by parties in those which have accepted it. For Englishmen to merely state that all the world are fools, because they are not convinced that the universal application of "Free Trade" would be an undoubted benefit, is merely insular conceit and prejudice. There must be serious reasons, which arise out of the different situations of continental and other nations, to cause these adverse opinions, besides the immense quantity of fallacies which are put forward sometimes seriously, sometimes speciously, by interested parties to prove the inadvisability of having no tariffs. Most of these are due to one or other of the following ideas.

It is often thought that the prosperity of special branches of industry is essential to a country, owing to reasons as often social or political, as economical; *e.g.*, agriculture in England at the beginning of the century, or manufactures in the United States of America now. This is furthered very greatly by the fact that the representatives of these industries are generally the most influential party in the land.

Again, it is believed that protection will enable a new industry, which otherwise would fail at the outset, to make a start and take its place as a normal development; and the only answer to this is that, as a matter of fact, this has seldom or never been the case.[1]

It is further held that taxes fall on the foreign importers and exporters, that tariffs are useful as a means of forcing concessions from other countries, and that recriminatory duties are justifiable and expedient.

It would be out of place to discuss the case here, but the historical bearing of the century's contest over this question is of the greatest importance. The gradual acceptance or refusal of Free Trade in this and other countries has been one of the chief moulding forces both of the quantity and nature of international trade.

England is indebted to Adam Smith for her early possession of Free Trade. His ideas, accepted by Pitt and other men of note at the end of the last century, were aided by the peculiar state of our manufactures and agriculture, already indicated, at the close of the French War. The large party, whose interests directly pointed to freedom, was continually reinforced, and, after a contest extending over thirty

[1] Sometimes when an industry has been thus fostered it has been at the expense of a more profitable trade. There is great difficulty in showing which of many causes has had most influence in launching a new manufacture. For instance, cotton-spinning in Bombay was assisted till 1882 by a small tax on imported manufactures, which caused much enterprise in the trade, and, to some extent, enabled it to obtain the position which it has since held. But the start would have been made in any case, and this artificial aid was responsible for unsound development and many business failures.

years, common prejudices and the opposition of the supreme agricultural party were overcome.

This position once accepted, the feeling against taxes on corn and on raw materials was so strong that, when Lord Derby's government, in 1852, proposed a new corn law, their term of office at once ended.

Triumphant in England, Free Trade for a short time appeared to carry all before it; in the seventh decade of this century commercial treaties were made with the Continent, and a great liberation of trade throughout the world ensued.

The first backward step was taken by the United States of America; the North and South War necessitated tariffs, hastily arranged to pay the war expenses. A great party, the Republicans, became committed to this system of revenue, and special interests, corruption, and national sentiment combined to prevent reductions of tariff.

In Europe also it was war that marked the time of reaction, but it was not the necessity of taxation that to any large extent caused the change. Free-trade ideas had never been thoroughly accepted on the Continent. The distress of France after the war made her the readier for what we should regard as quack remedies; every effort was made to imitate England's industrial success by encouraging home manufactures as the best way of rendering the nation prosperous. In Germany, the opposite cause produced the same effect. The unnatural and spurious prosperity which followed the payment of the French war indemnity of £20,000,000 gave the start to manufacturing industries, which soon proved to be on an unsound basis.

In the reaction that followed these had to be supported by protective tariffs.

There was a further cause of a more general nature. The advocates of Free Trade had exaggerated its benefits and power, almost promising that a millennium of peace and prosperity would follow its general adoption. Unfortunately, nearly every country in the world was engaged in war some time between 1854 and 1877. A great depression of trade, ruinous to merchants, began in 1873, from which the recovery was very slow. The case for Free Trade was reconsidered; tariffs were again imposed. In America the idea that the States could and should produce everything they required, making an isolated world for themselves, had great influence; and, generally, the object-lesson which England presented of prosperity following manufactures, induced other countries to try to imitate her special circumstances rather than her general methods.

New countries, such as Australia and New Zealand, have also this hankering after mines and manufactures, with the idea that, started under protection, they will in their growth be able to dispense with it.

Only Holland, Belgium,[1] and New South Wales[2] agree with England in full acceptance of Free Trade. For England the peculiar nature of her trade renders it a necessity, and there is little fear of any powerful reaction at home.

Our immediate purpose is to trace the battle and the victory of Free Trade in the middle of this century.

[1] See p. 151 for amendment.

[2] Since Jan. 1, 1901, merged with the rest of Australia.

3. ENGLAND'S ADOPTION OF FREE TRADE.

It was not the theory of Free Trade, but the practical need that impelled the London and Edinburgh merchants to petition, in 1820, against "every restrictive regulation of trade not essential to the revenue." A commission was appointed in response to these petitions, and they found that as regards revenue there were an infinite number of petty duties serving no purpose but to hinder trade, and laid down the fundamental principle that:—"Commerce must be a source of reciprocal amity between nations, and an interchange of productions to promote the industry, the wealth and the happiness of mankind," and, "if we should be compelled to continue any of the present restrictions . . . . it will be understood . . . . that it is a matter not of option, but of necessity, and not caused by any ideas on our part of promoting our own commercial interests by it." The liberality of these sentences and of the ensuing policy, coming at the close of a war which had burdened us with a debt greater than any nation had previously borne, when revenue was of the highest importance, and any experiments therewith of the greatest risks, forms a striking contrast to the action of the Americans in 1866, and of the French in 1873, when similar circumstances induced them to raise their tariff in order to recoup their exchequers.

This commission was appointed in 1820. The Corn Laws were not repealed till 1846; for though the case had been thus clearly stated, and the opinion of experts given, the confusion of the country after the war and the one-sided views that distress generates clouded the issue; different claims were raised by classes with conflicting interests, and amid the uproar the old-established monopolies only yielded their ground step by step.

Newmarch's description of our fiscal system in 1820 is as follows:—"At that time the system of prohibition, protection and fiscal confusion was at its height. It was said by competent authorities that the number of Acts of Parliament relating to the entry, export and custody of goods as matters of Custom House supervision, was not less than fifteen hundred. All the special interests were in full possession of the vested rights to which they laid claim. There was the Corn Law of 1815;[1] there were the differential duties in favour of the West India proprietors; the monopoly of the East India Company; the rigorous application of the navigation laws against competition on freights. There were heavy duties on raw materials of industry, and prohibitive or extravagant duties on foreign manufactures."

Mr. Huskisson, in spite of opposition, made the first inroad on this system while President of the Board of Trade from 1823 to 1827,[2] during which four years our imports increased 26 per cent., the tariff on raw silk was reduced from 5s. 7½d. to 1d., on raw wool from 6d. to 1d., on manufactured from 50 to 15 per cent., and the prohibition on silk manufactures was

[1] Prohibiting the importation of wheat when the price was under 80s., and rendering it free when above 80s.

[2] See Leone Levi's "History of British Commerce," pp. 172-3.

changed to a duty of 30 per cent.; other similar reductions were made, and the commercial union of Great Britain and Ireland was completed.

After this there was a pause in fiscal legislation for twelve years, during which our imports increased 50 per cent. and our exports 40 per cent. (real value), the increment made in Mr. Huskisson's Presidency being thus maintained.

Then came the second period of reform, Mr. Peel's administration, culminating in the repeal of the Corn Laws.

In 1840, a committee, known as "Hume's committee," had reported that "The tariff of the United Kingdom presents neither congruity nor unity of purpose; it often aims at incompatible ends. The duties are sometimes meant to be both productive of revenue and for protection. Whilst the tariff has been made subordinate to many small-producing interests at home by the sacrifice of revenue, in order to support their interests, the same principle of interference is largely applied by the various discriminating duties to the produce of our colonies, by which exclusive advantages are given to the colonial interests at the expense of the mother country." In 1842 there were 1,090 articles charged with duties, many of them barely repaying the costs of collection.

Villiers was the first parliamentary champion of the attack on the Corn Laws. Every year from 1838 onwards he moved against an overwhelming majority a resolution for their revision. At about the same time Richard Cobden, soon to be joined by John Bright, gave his attention to the subject, and in

1839 the Anti-corn-law League[1] was initiated at Manchester.

The report of Hume's committee was taken as their text-book. The press issued a continuous flow of pamphlets which were energetically distributed. All over the country the discussion was carried on with the greatest vigour. Public meetings were held in every county in the teeth of the fiercest opposition, but the League was enthusiastically welcomed, and, more than once, an audience, hostile at the commencement of the meeting, were almost unanimously in favour of the resolutions at the end.

In 1842 and 1845, Peel made great reductions in duties, especially on raw materials, most of which were allowed to be imported free. The export of machinery was at last recognised, and foreign manufactures admitted at reduced duties.

Between 1840 and 1847, imports increased 34 per cent. and exports 44 per cent. in value, while in spite of these immense remissions of duties the increasing trade kept excise and customs at their old level.

The Protectionist party, beaten in argument, and confuted by the reviving prosperity of the country, gave all their strength to the defence of the Corn Laws, but the time had at last come for their repeal.

With the object-lesson of bad harvests and high prices before them, the people at large were determined to have cheap corn. Peel himself was convinced by the facts, and, though he was returned in 1842 with a majority of 91 pledged to defend the Corn Laws, the majority diminished, the Government

[1] At first called the Anti-corn-law Association.

resigned in 1845, and Peel came back pledged for their repeal. The League had won; all its prominent members were seated in the House, and the Corn Laws were abolished by a majority of 97.

The same Parliament introduced further reforms in tariff. Amongst these the sugar question was attacked: differential duties had been levied on imported sugar, the West Indies were favoured more than the East Indies, and both more than other countries, so that the duties on sugar from these three sources were respectively 14s., 17s. 6d., 21s. 6d., for the same quantity; but in 1848 the duties were equalised. Our carrying trade was thrown open to all nations by the repeal of the Navigation Laws in 1849. The finishing touches to the perfection of our Free Trade system were put by Mr. Gladstone in 1852, since which time duties have only been levied, purely for purposes of revenue, on some dozen articles which cannot be produced at home.[1]

4. THE IMMEDIATE EFFECTS OF FREE TRADE.

Turning from the method in which these reforms were effected, let us trace their results on the wealth of the people.

In the first place, there is no reason to suppose that wages or incomes as a whole rose or fell to any great extent between 1815 and 1850; but prices, and therefore the purchasing power of money, varied greatly.

[1] A small duty remained till 1849. From 1849 to 1869 a so-called registration duty of 1s. a quarter was imposed on all grain, and a similar duty existed in 1902-3.

From 1820-1835 prices were considerably lower than during the war; owing to favourable seasons at home, to improvements in manufacture and scientific agriculture, to a low rate of interest, to the relief from the dangers of exporting and importing goods in open warfare, and to Mr. Huskisson's reductions of duty.[1] Prices ranged a little higher in the next few years, but began to fall steadily in 1841. The evidence which the index number affords is very striking. The date of Peel's first reforms is the date of the commencement of the fall, and as in successive years trade after trade was liberated, prices decreased regularly till 1851, after the influx of Australian and Californian gold was felt.

The index number changes from 103 in 1840 to 75 in 1851: *i.e.*, £75 in 1851 went as far as £103 in 1840, whilst incomes and wages had slightly increased.

The prices of certain imports (duties deducted) at those dates are:—

Years.	Wheat.	Coffee.	Years.	Tea.
1840	£3 6s. 4d. per quarter	84s. per cwt.	1839	1s. 7d. per lb.
1850	£2 0s. 3d. ,,	36s. ,,	1851	1s. 1d. ,,

Years.	Sugar.	Butter (Irish).	Raw Silk.
1840	40s. 0d. per cwt.	90s. per cwt.	18s. per lb.
1850	24s. 6d. ,,	70s. ,,	16s. ,,

Years.	Cotton Wool.	Merino Wool.
1840	5d. per lb.	2s. 1d. per lb.
1850	5½d. ,,	1s. 5d. ,,

[1] *Vide* Tooke's "History of Prices."

In 1885, when the index number is nearly the same as in 1850, prices were:—

Wheat.	Coffee.	Tea.	Sugar.	Silk.	Cotton.	Wool.
£1 12s. 10d.	61s.	1s. 2d.	14s. per cwt.	14s.	5d.	10d.

It is important to notice exactly how this reduction was brought about in this period when no other country was free-trading, and we were the world's manufacturers. Duties on imports and exports were removed; the reduction of price made a greater demand at home for imports, and abroad for exports. The output of the factories was therefore increased, methods were improved, economies due to work on a large scale adopted; we had a monopoly abroad, and the same labour more efficiently applied producing a larger output, more foreign goods were obtained in return.

At the same time, while in 1830-1840 5 per cent. of the population were fed on foreign corn, in 1840-1850 the percentage was 12 per cent. Hence a smaller proportion of labourers were employed on the unproductive work of cultivating inferior soil. The price of wheat fell 40 per cent; it could not possibly pay to continue the ploughing of steep hills, stiff clay or stony ground. The labour formerly so employed had to seek new work; the diminution (relative and actual) of the population of the agricultural counties, and the increase in the northern, show how this labour was used. Railways were constructed, factories and workshops built, and machinery set up; that is, surplus labour was invested in fixed capital which would bring profit in the next decade. And while thus increasing our capital, and laying the foundations of new work, the factory "hands" in the north, and the miners and iron-workers, were with the product of comparatively little labour buying food for the whole of England, the result of long tedious toil of peasants on the Continent, and colonists in new countries, who thought themselves well paid by our manufactures.

IV.—SUCCESS OF FREE TRADE, 1850-1870.

1. UNLIMITED EXPANSION.

THE almost unlimited expansion which becomes marked about 1850 and culminates in 1873 has been pointed to by many different people as proof of the great effect of different measures or inventions; as a matter of fact, it was due to no one cause, but was rather the result of multitudinous discoveries and events, acting and reacting on each other. Perhaps the following list of dates[1] shows this most clearly:—

Opening of first English railway, ...	1830
Wheatstone's telegraph, ...	1837
First ocean steamer, ...	1838
Settlement in New Zealand, ...	1840
Reduction of duties on raw materials, ...	1842
Repeal of Corn Laws, ...	1846
Commercial treaty with France, ...	1860

Here are seven events of widely different natures, each of which must have had its effect in the period under consideration, and it would be useless, even if it were possible, to weigh the separate result of each. We cannot estimate, we can obtain no criterion of the vast effects of the adoption of Free Trade. Three things, however, are clear:—First, that till the

[1] For completer list, *vide* pp. ix. x.

suffocating restrictions were removed, trade could not expand; when exports were prohibited, imports could not be plentiful; when imports were taxed, the demand at enhanced prices could not be great. Secondly, if every restriction was removed from every branch of trade, there would be no increase without natural causes of manufacture and demand, no increased demand without a cheapening or improvement of supply; that, in fact, Free Trade is the method, not the source, of commerce, and that the claim of this increase as the direct result of freedom and a proof of its expediency is an inaccurate exaggeration. Thirdly, that the date of the marked commencement of the expansion coincides exactly with the reductions and abolitions of duties,[1] pointing to the fact, borne out by all concurrent events, that the adoption of Free Trade was the opening of the valve which allowed the forces of commerce full play.

Let us consider of what nature these forces were.

The underlying cause, without which the others would have been futile, was the great increase of human efficiency (*i.e.*, of the quantity of useful goods which the same effort could produce) owing to the use of machinery, and the general adaptation of science to production. "Men are multiplied a hundred and a thousandfold,"[2] as William Morris puts it, and thus more wealth is produced, more has to be

[1] The financial reforms were from 1842-1852. In Diagrams i. and iv., the slope of the upper curve, which shows the rate of increase, becomes steeper from 1842-1852.

[2] "Dream of John Ball."

DIAGRAM IV.

showing expansion of trade: 1830 - 1873.

A Value of Imports & Exports together C Exports (including re exports)
B Imports. [change in method of valuation in 1854]

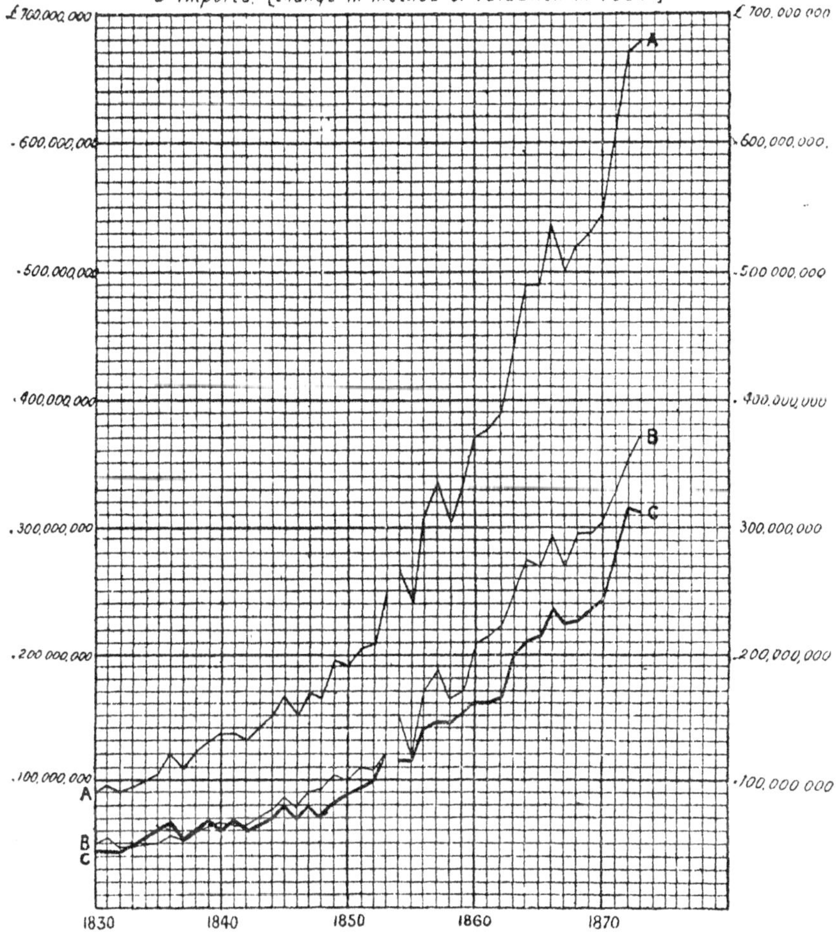

distributed, and as each trade increases its output, it is necessary to find a wider area of customers.

Again, the very nature of this change caused specialisation; each man worked at one detail of his trade, each town and district became the home of special manufactures, and the next step was that the work of each country was specialised. It is true that at the period of which we are speaking, these special trades were new discoveries of the land which made them its own, and the old industries went on as before; but it was in the trades of comparatively recent establishment, in England especially, that there were immense outputs (of cotton goods and machinery, for instance), in great excess of the home demand; and this could only pay if the foreign demand grew in proportion to the growing efficiency; that is to say, our newer industries became the more important, and were marked as our division of international labour.

The foreign demand, indeed, for our manufactures and our machines was extraordinary. Now, every country is trying to rival our goods, and each to produce for herself the manufactures she requires; then, rivalry was out of the question.

During the war, in spite of all restrictions, and of penal laws in force even against possessors of British goods, we had found a large market on the Continent. In the first quarter of the century evidence was given to a Parliamentary Commission[1] of the powerlessness of the Customs House to stop the exportation of machinery, and of artisans to set it up. The exportation being prohibited, parts of machines were packed

[1] Select Committee on Artisans and Machinery, 1824.

separately, or different machines mixed together so that it was impossible to identify them, or a forbidden press would be exported among old iron. The demand was such that every risk was well rewarded.

At the date we have reached, England was especially to the fore in railway construction. £150,000,000 were invested in English railways between 1846 and 1850, the money coming from the middle classes [1] without disorganising the trade of the country, or hindering our progress in other directions. Our railways were immediately the envy of the Continent. Engineers, navvies, and steel were sent abroad *en masse.* For instance, in 1842 Mr. Brassey took a colony of 4,000 navvies to build the railway from Paris to Rouen, and these gave the French labourers their first lesson in railway construction. Man for man, the English earned twice as much as the French; but after a time on other railways the French were found the more skilful in certain parts of the work, while the dangerous and hard work continued to require English hardihood. At later dates labourers were also exported (in many ways the effect on trade being the same as from the exportation of goods) to construct the Grand Trunk Railway in Canada and a line in New South Wales.

In 1845, Belgium, Germany and France had together 7,000 miles, and the United States 9,000 miles of railway laid down or projected.

The end of this period, viz., the years 1868-72, shows another great increase in railways, definitely marked, too, in the increase of iron, steel, machinery

[1] Tooke's "History of Prices."

and other goods, which at that date we were exporting as capital on loan to foreign countries.

Railways were thus extended all over the world. Many of the undertakings and investments were speculative and rash. In England, in 1849, the capital invested had depreciated to half the value of the actual money paid. Yet though the investors did not reap the full reward, the railways were there, and soon brought their natural benefits to the world at large.

On every side new markets were opened; old trades were increased, new developed. The railways built with our materials opened up districts hitherto inaccessible; this acted as a fresh stimulus to our manufacturers—more capital was forthcoming, and more railways were built.

Not only were countries, with which we had already established some trade, brought nearer and in closer relation, but new countries were discovered. Australia and New Zealand were ready to take our surplus population, and were not behindhand in the new system of development. Our older colonies also increased. With each emigration the number of our customers abroad was multiplied.

In 1850 and 1852 this process was accelerated by the news of the gold discoveries in California and Australia. So great was the emigration and the consequent demand for ships that all freights were increased, and, with a short lull, this continued till 1856 Immense quantities of manufactures went to pay for the influx of gold, and a great impulse was given to the shipbuilding trade.

Meanwhile population was increasing with great rapidity. The census returns show—

For 1831 . .	16,400,000	in England and Wales.
,, 1841 . .	18,600,000	
,, 1851 . .	20,900,000	
,, 1861 . .	23,300,000	
,, 1871 . .	26,200,000	

These numbers could not have been supported in England before these developments, and the fact that they were living in greater comfort than their fathers is proof at once of the magnitude and the advantages of our foreign trade.

The last great impetus was given by the Suez Canal, by which the journey to India and the East was quickened by one-half, and, at the same time, rendered more secure. Its great effect in modifying the courses of trade—an effect particularly felt in England—will be considered in another place.[1] In the present connection we notice that just as railways rendered profitable the exchange of commodities that hitherto distance had rendered almost inconceivable, and had also stimulated all other trades in which the item of distance was considerable, so the Canal made India and Europe neighbours, who could serve each other to great advantage.

It must suffice to mention the telegraph, with its later rival, the telephone, as serving the same ends; by diminishing the time necessary to complete an exchange, they have great effect in curtailing the supply that must be kept in stock to provide for

[1] *Vide* p. 71.

a continued demand, with the consequent release of capital, and the partial displacement of the "middle-man."

While Free Trade between nations was allowing these inventions and enterprises their natural swing, the concurrent development of free competition at home was stimulating our manufacturers to use to the full every means of saving labour, increasing output and diminishing cost.

Everything went to show that the same laws govern internal and international trade; there was every promise of a long era of increasing freedom and increasing prosperity.

2. TREATIES WITH FOREIGN COUNTRIES.

While Mr. Gladstone was completing Peel's reforms at home, Cobden was travelling in Europe, making an almost royal progress. Educated continental opinion was waking to the fact that the system of trade then in vogue was neither logical nor successful. When all dogmas were challenged at the time of the revolutions of 1848, the economic dogmas received their share of criticism. The campaign in England, then as now connected with the name of Cobden, was watched with interest; and when the hero of the fight crossed to Europe, in each country he was received by the men of most original or advanced opinions with enthusiasm. In Italy, Prussia, France and Russia, he was closeted with emperors, kings or statesmen, to whom he expounded the new theory of trade. His personality, as well as his logic, always obtained for him a sympathetic audience, and it was entirely by his personal influence that the celebrated commercial treaty between England and France was arranged.

In accepting Free Trade, England had not anticipated that Europe would follow her example. In his speech in 1844, Peel had said: "I have no guarantee that other countries will immediately follow our example—it is a fact that other countries have not followed our example, and have levied higher duties in some cases on our goods . . . . I rely on that fact as a conclusive proof of the policy of the course we are pursuing[1] . . . . But depend upon it, your example will ultimately prevail. When your example could be quoted in favour of restriction it was quoted largely. When your example can be quoted in favour of relaxation . . . . reason and common sense will induce relaxation of high duties."

Nevertheless, by accidental circumstances, political convenience or a partial acceptance of the logic of trade, considerable progress had been made before Cobden's treaty. Sardinia, Switzerland, Holland and Portugal had become free-traders before 1854. Austria, Prussia and neighbouring States had arranged a common tariff by mutual concessions. The Zollverein, Austria, Belgium, Spain, Russia, Denmark and Sweden, had reduced their tariffs for political reasons.

Then the great impetus was given by the treaty between England and France; and between 1859

[1] In another sentence he explains that it is hopeless to wait till concessions can be obtained, and that England must have freedom of trade, alone in opposition to the world, or not at all.

and 1865 treaties were concluded with Belgium, Germany,[1] Russia, Sweden and Norway, Italy and Austria, while many of these countries also made treaties with each other. In most cases there was a "most favoured nation" clause by which we were entitled to every reduction made or advantage granted to any other nation. For instance, France could not, under the terms of the treaty, admit German manufactures on more favourable terms than ours.[2]

Great as was the advance which these treaties indicated, they were only the first step in the direction of Free Trade, and the second step still remains to be taken; for duties were not abolished, except in rare cases; our goods were admitted, but under a maximum tariff of 30 per cent., while foreign goods were allowed free entry to England.

Naturally, our trade with these countries increased greatly. In the years 1860 and 1870, our imports and exports from and to the following countries were—

	France.		Germany, Holland and Belgium.	
	Imports.	Exports.	Imports.	Exports.
1860	£18 million	£5 million	£40 million	£20 million
1870	38 ,,	12 ,,	45 ,,	37 ,,

Our total imports and exports increased 50 per cent. in the ten years, while international trade on the Continent increased to an almost fabulous extent;

[1] The Zollverein.

[2] "Each of the two high contracting powers engages to confer on the other any favour, privilege, or reduction in the tariff of duties of importation on the articles mentioned in the present treaty which the said power may concede to any third power."

that of the countries which were benefiting by the system of treaties (which gave at once to all each advantage granted to any) was doubled. Enterprise and general vigour and prosperity followed all over Europe, and the general causes which were increasing efficiency in work and intimacy in trade brought the commerce of non-free-trading countries also to two-thirds as much again as in 1860.

There was no general change in prices at this period, but the prosperity of trade was shown by rising wages.

Between 1860 and 1870 wages rose on an average about 12 per cent., and the income of the nation per head of the population 25 per cent. All classes appear to have received some benefit. It is estimated that wages in agriculture rose 7 per cent., in Scotch mining about the same, in the Building Trades 16 per cent., in Engineering 10 per cent., in Iron and Steel manufacture 27 per cent., and in Cotton factories 25 per cent.

As before, we cannot distinguish which were the causes and which the results of this improvement, but our home trade could not have increased without the enlarged markets open to us, nor would these have been opened except by the more liberal views which produced international treaties of commerce and peace.

3. AMERICAN WAR AND ITS EFFECTS—TRADE WITH THE UNITED STATES AND INDIA.

A glance at the import figures of the years 1850-1870 shows that some great disorganisation of trade took place between 1860 and 1868; and the details show that the fluctuations were in the cotton industry, and relate to the United States and to India.[1]

The war between the Northern and Southern States, in 1861-5, had very striking and far-reaching effects on trade in many directions. During that time intercourse with the States was suspended, and the result showed at once the importance to England of the cotton trade, the closeness of our relations with the States, and, further, that the market for corn had become so wide that the effect on prices of a war in the country of our greatest supply was very slight.

Our cotton imports in the years 1860-1870 were—

Year.	Weight. (00,000,000 lbs.)	Value. (millions)
1860	14	£35
1861	12	40
1862	4	30
1863	7	55
1864	9	75
1865	10	65
1866	14	70
1867	13	50
1868	13	55
1869	20	57
1870	13	52

Thus our *supply* was greatly diminished in 1860 to 1864, while the *price* increased immensely. The suffering in Manchester caused by this cotton famine is well known, as also are the exciting tales of blockade-running, by which some small quantities of cotton

[1] *Vide* Diagrams iv., vii., x.

were obtained, and the Americans supplied at fabulous prices with our goods.

During these years the values of our imports of all kinds from India and the Levant (including Egypt, Turkey, etc.), were—

Year.	India.	Levant.
1860	£18 millions	£15 millions
1861	25 "	15 "
1862	38 "	15 "
1863	53 "	20 "
1864	55 "	25 "
1865	43 "	28 "
1866	40 "	22 "
1867	30 "	20 "
1868	35 "	25 "
1869	40 "	27 "
1870	30 "	22 "

These figures show clearly the development of new cotton fields, which sprang up as if by magic in response to the demand. Before the war was over, and long before America had recovered from the strain, India and Egypt had grown and sent to us a new crop, which, in 1865, nearly reached the former normal supply. The influences of high prices and ready enterprise effected this unprecedented growth of a new trade. The elasticity and adaptability of the world's labour, which rapid communication and increasing intercourse had rendered possible, has never been so well shown as at this time.

We also see the evils which the same causes may bring in their train.

Owing to our dependence on the people of another

continent, an unexpected rebellion, a new political party or a change in fiscal laws over which we have no possible control, may paralyse our trade, throw thousands of hands out of work, and have an effect which may almost be compared with that caused in the old times of non-intercourse by an insufficient harvest.

Moreover, sudden fluctuations of this nature give rise to speculative purchases, which may ruin or make the fortune of a merchant as chance decides, and to the initiation or increase of new sources and methods of making up the old supply, which on the return of normal trade will be found to have no solid basis, will have to be relinquished at a loss, and cause further disturbances. Thus, in the present instance, though cotton growth, having been developed in such abnormal conditions in India, has proved a stable and profitable trade, the profits to be made from this investment were so much exaggerated that several companies over-committed themselves and in the reaction failed; the "Glasgow Bank" failed in 1878 from this cause, ten years after the events, and by so doing aggravated a further commercial crisis.

These, however, are the evils of the *growth* of foreign trade, not of its perfect development, and they carry their remedy with them. The supply of cotton is now so wide that disturbances must occur in the same year in both hemispheres to produce any very great effect. [See Note 4, p. 151.]

The effects of the war on American finance were most disastrous from the Free Trade point of view.

There had been a reaction from the high tariff of

1830 already mentioned. The Southern States then, as now, agricultural, while the Northern were partly manufacturing, opposed the tariff, and a successive reduction to be completed in 1842 was arranged. During this time (1829 to 1836) our exports increased from five to twelve millions; another severe depression (in England as well as America), however, enabled the protectionists to return to the tariff of 1832.

In 1846, Secretary Walker's scheme reduced duties to an average of 25 per cent., and another substantial reduction followed in 1857. Just before the war the duties were only 14 per cent. on total imports, the average for the past twenty years having been about 20 per cent. But between 1861 and 1863 tariffs were altogether doubled, recklessly, to meet war expenses, and further increased to a maximum of 46 per cent. in 1868. These tariffs have been changed again and again to suit the party predominant for the time being, and have never been substantially reduced. Our exports have accordingly shown the most violent fluctuations, having hardly (except in the inflation of 1870-1873) exceeded the £30,000,000, which was the figure for 1866, nor increased at all since 1880. Finally, the McKinley tariff of 1890 taxes imports 29 per cent. *ad valorem* on the average. [See Note 3, p. 150.]

Within two years a reaction against McKinley has followed; the "Democrats" have been returned, and the tariff is to be reduced. In March, 1893, President Cleveland told his fellow-citizens that they "could not defy with impunity the inexorable laws of finance and trade." All abuses, revenue from tariff not required by the State, pensions, combinations, are to be remedied, and he continues: "While there should be no surrender of principle, our task must be undertaken wisely, without vindictiveness. Our mission is not punishment, but the rectification of wrongs. If in lifting the burdens from the daily life of our people we reduce inordinate and unequal advantages too long enjoyed, this is but a necessary incident of our return to right and justice. If we exact from unwilling minds acquiescence in the theory of an honest distribution of the fund of governmental beneficence treasured up for all, we but insist upon the principle which underlies our free institutions. When we tear aside the delusions and misconceptions which have blinded our countrymen to their condition under vicious tariff laws, we but show them how far they have been led away from the paths of contentment and prosperity. When we proclaim that necessity for revenue to support Government furnishes the only justification for taxing the people, we announce a truth so plain that its denial would seem to indicate the extent to which judgment may be influenced by familiarity with perversions of taxing power; and when we seek to reinstate the self-confidence and business enterprise of our citizens by discrediting abject dependence upon the governmental favour, we strive to stimulate those elements of American character which support the hope of American achievements."

This cannot, however, be regarded as a final settlement of the dispute. The tariff will not be so far reduced that it will resemble the English system; nor is the "Republican" party destroyed. [See Note 3, p. 150.]

It is in the United States that the Free Trade battle is being fought out for the edification of the world. They have the greatest advantages from the Protectionist point of view. The republic is so vast, the population and the climate so varied, that it already produces part of all the different goods they require, and is almost a world in itself. Considering the room there still is for the increase of population to adjust itself to requirements, in the future they might reduce their foreign trade to almost nothing, as they at one time reduced their merchant navy, and the loss would be less to them than to any other community, while their wealth may well continue to increase and conceal the deficit.

The Americans have the English qualifications for work, and in most of our manufactures our advantage is only differential, that is, we have some one quality in a slightly greater degree than they. Their mineral resources are still partially unknown, and it is possible that in the not very distant future they may need all the corn they grow, and so not require an outlet for it.

However, it is not the American's declared intention to separate himself from the rest of the world; his hope is to tax the foreigner and sustain no loss himself. The McKinley and former tariffs should have gone far to undeceive him; the southern farmers find that they are being taxed, and though a tariff has been fixed on imported agricultural produce, they are not satisfied; the opposition party is very strong, and if anything occurs to make America too poor to afford her present waste, Free Traders may continue to enjoy the triumph which the recent elections have begun. [See note 3, p. 150.]

This is a suitable place for noticing the gradual development of Indian trade.

Our exports to India have shown a very regular progression during the whole of the century. The East Indian Company did more harm by monopolising the trade outside their immediate territory, by selling goods in England at unreasonable prices, and exacting privileges vexatious and hurtful to other traders, than by neglecting to develop the resources of India; and it was chiefly because the interests committed to it were becoming too vast for private management that the repeal of its charter became necessary in 1833.

India and our colonies have commercially some points in common. Both have been useful and regular markets for our special manufactures, cotton and machinery; and both, without injury to our trade, have availed themselves of the permission granted to them in 1822-1825 to trade with other countries.

The Suez Canal had a great effect in altering the direction of Indian trade. European countries began to import direct from India; and whereas in 1871 £30,000,000 worth of goods was exported to England out of a total of £57,000,000 worth, in 1887 the values were £25,500,000 and £66,000,000, and in 1900 £22,500,000 out of £78,000,000.

Our trade, however, is not really diminished, for India received two-thirds of her imports from us in 1900, and payment is made indirectly.

The use of jute as a substitute for hemp in coarse mattings, bags, etc., has since 1860 given to India a large and steady trade, and to England another manufacture. India, England, and the Continent compete in the manufacture, and the raw material reaches the Continent both directly and through England.

India's cotton trade, though long in existence, received its great impetus from the American War, and was then firmly established. So great were India's gains at that time that she obtained enough money and credit to import iron from us in large quantities and develop her present railway system. The inflation was exaggerated, and the interest of the debt then contracted has been a burden.

Raw cotton is still exported from India, while the manufactured goods are imported; but now the nearness of the raw material, the cheapness of labour, and the extent of the demand in the neighbourhood, are making it profitable to manufacture on the spot. The relative advantages of Indian labour in the heat, and that of the skilled Englishman in his own climate, have still, however, to be decided.[1] A new and important factor in Indian trade has recently been introduced by the discovery of extensive fields of coal in India, which is likely to have marked effect on her manufacturing power. The production in 1899 was 4,900,000 tons.

[1] *Vide* VI. 1 *infra*.

DIAGRAM V,
showing Excess of Imports, 1855-1903.

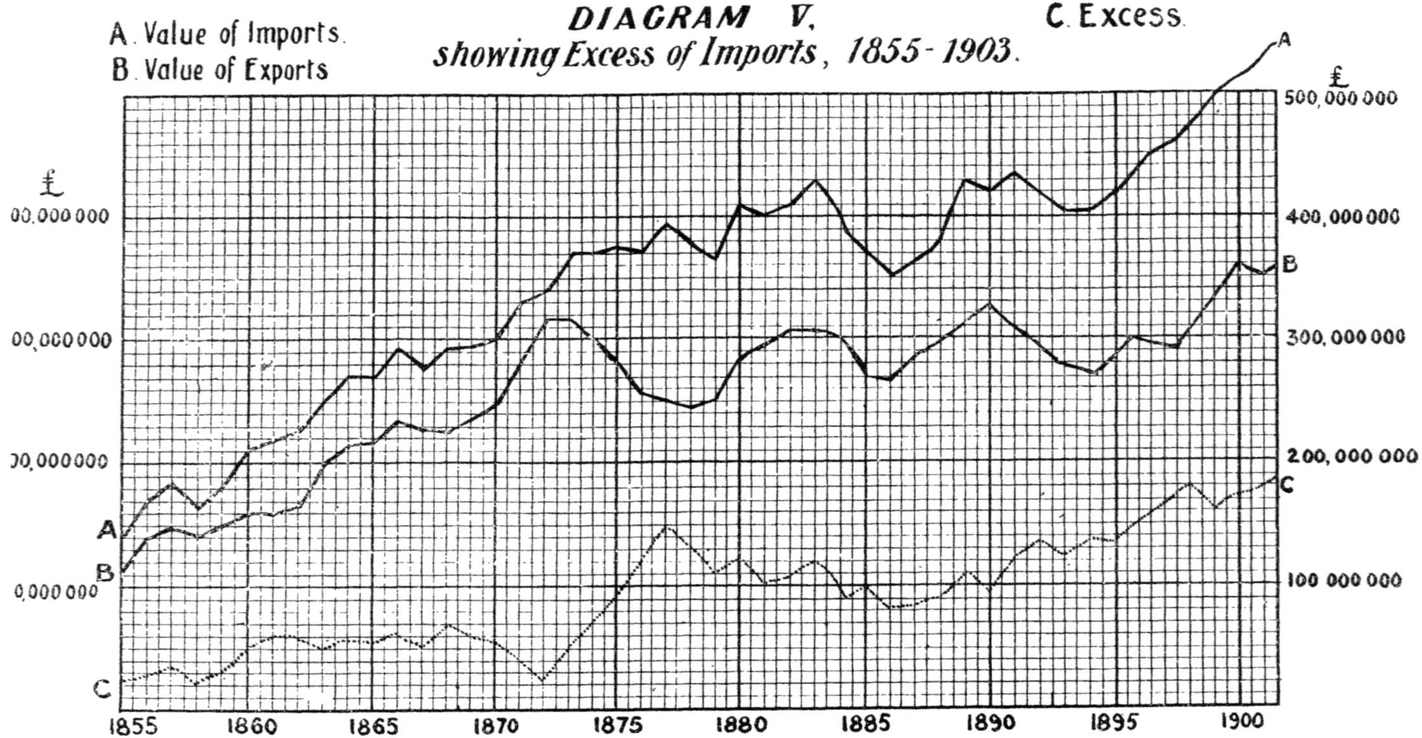

4. BALANCE OF IMPORTS AND EXPORTS—ENGLAND'S FOREIGN INVESTMENTS.

It is a maxim of Free Traders that exports and imports pay for each other; and this, when rightly interpreted, is strictly true.

But the most casual glance at a diagram shows the marked and growing excess of imports over exports since 1855. This is due partly to the interest paid by other countries on our loans to them, which income was estimated as nearly £90,000,000 in 1900, and partly to the earnings of our shipping.

The countries with which we trade may conveniently be divided into three classes: those who receive from us in imports more than they return in exports; those who receive and return the same quantity; and, the largest class, those who return more than they receive.

No country has been long in the first class, and no country of importance is now in it. But from 1868 to 1875 Germany was taking great quantities of exports, from which it appears that some of the war indemnity paid by France was advanced by us, and as we should expect, France was repaying us in the following years, when her imports to us were large.

At the time of the gold discoveries imports into Australia were largely in excess of exports, being paid for in gold, not goods.

As our Colonies and the more backward countries have developed, they have passed from the first class, through the second, and into the third. In the early stages we exported goods on loan; after a certain period the interest payable on these loans becomes greater than new capital sent out, and so the normal condition is reached, in which an excess of the goods they send over those they receive pays for the services of our ships. South Africa is still in the first class; Canada has long been in the third; Australia and India have fluctuated near the second; South America has recently reached the third.

In the third class we find the United States, Germany, Russia, France, Holland, Belgium, and India. The excess is most marked in the case of the United States, and is a striking illustration of the effect of a high tariff, for our exports have decreased, and our imports thence are paid for by circular trade through India, China, and other countries. Thus, the whole exports of the States have greatly exceeded their imports in recent years, but their imports from the West Indies, Chili, Brazil, China, Japan, and France exceed their exports to those countries.

Our shipping figures throw some light on this. Since 1832 we have done half the carrying trade of the States, and a large fraction of it in former times; 13 per cent. of our vessels are employed in this trade. The same applies to our trade with Russia, Germany, and France, from whom we probably earned 5, 6, and 11 millions respectively in 1883, and a similar sum from Holland. [These statements may not apply to 1905.]

There is still a large sum to be accounted for in connection with the United States, Russia, and

France; we must be receiving from them great sums of interest in return for capital lent in the two great periods of railway mania and at other times.

From India we received goods of great value at the time of the cotton famine; now we receive interest on loans, and the balance is complicated by special causes.

Generally, the balance of the nominal values of our imports and exports is governed by the following factors:—

All capital which is sent abroad goes in the form of exports: all interest on this capital returns in the form of imports.

Our ships do a large fraction of the carrying trade of the world, and thus pay annually for some £90,000,000[1] worth of imports.

It is possible to correct the total figures of imports and exports for the earnings of shipping and many smaller causes, and a considerable excess of imports remain, which represents the interest paid on capital abroad, less the amount of capital freshly exported. Thus, if we exported capital exactly equal to the value of the interest due to us, this excess of imports would be nothing, as was the case in 1873 and 1886. If more capital were sent abroad than interest returned, exports would be in excess, as in 1859, 1872, and other years; if, as has generally been the case since 1860, imports (thus corrected for shipping, etc.) are in excess, we are receiving interest from abroad in excess of capital sent out.

[1] The exact figure is not known: this is the estimate adopted by the Board of Trade in 1903 (Cd. 1761, p. 101).

For instance, in 1880 imports actually exceeded exports by £122,000,000. Some £70,000,000 paid for the services of English ships, and other minor causes, reduced the excess to £45,000,000. Apparently, in that year, there was about £1,500,000,000 of English capital abroad, paying about 5 per cent. on an average. Thus £75,000,000 was due for interest. £45,000,000 only was received, and therefore about £30,000,000 was left abroad for re-investment.[1]

The figures give no obvious means of deciding actually how much interest returned, and how much capital was newly invested, they only show the excess of the former over the latter; but by close scrutiny (as explained in note at end of chapter) the actual values can approximately be found.[2]

It appears that before 1854 we had some £550,000,000 invested abroad, in Government loans and railways presumably. Increasing annual investments, averaging £30,000,000 per annum, which would largely take the form of machinery and stock for railways, and manufactures, which would pay the wages of the labourers employed in their construction, brought the total in 1860 to about £750,000,000.

During the cotton crisis slightly less capital appears to have been invested; but from 1870-1875, during

[1] More accurately, £75,000,000 interest was received, while £30,000,000 new capital was invested.

[2] The figures given so far are due to Mr. Giffen's well-known investigations, interpreted by recognised estimates. The figures which follow are new, and not so reliable, but agree with all available facts, and appear to be the only ones consistent with them.

the great inflation before and after the Franco-Prussian War, some £55,000,000 annually brought the total to not much less than £1,400,000,000. A reaction followed, and for three years there was very little investment, but from 1881 to 1890, it seems not improbable that £600,000,000, was added, and the total brought to £2,000,000,000.[1]

We have thus additional evidence of the great investments in railways which took place in 1871 and 1872; of the growing confidence in international securities; of the increased saving that made these investments possible, and of the effect a commercial depression has in checking enterprise. We also see that (if the figures are to be trusted) the depression of 1886-88 was not marked by a fall, but rather by an increase in capital invested (unless a sudden and heavy fall in interest took place just at that time), which confirms the impression that this crisis was not accompanied by any great fall in the volume of trade transacted.

Great as has been the benefit which England has conferred both on her colonies and on nearly all the foreign nations of the world in supplying them with £2,000,000,000, which her industry and genius enabled her to spare, she has not been altogether blameless in her transactions. Her capital was so tempting to the foreigner, and, since capital invested in foreign railways almost always extended her trade and reacted to her benefit, so easy for them to obtain, that nation

[1] More reliance may be placed on the relative rates of increase than on the actual figures. The total can hardly be estimated accurately within 25 per cent.

after nation has borrowed more than they were able to use or could afford to repay. Great nations, like Russia and Germany,[1] were spendthrifts, in 1873, with our capital, Russia especially launching into enterprises which crippled her resources. The United States have speculated with our capital. Semi-civilised nations, as the Turks and Greeks, have over-borrowed and repudiated their debt, after, however, the original investors had more than repaid their outlay by a few years' exorbitant interest. India has borrowed, and at one time was borrowing again to pay the interest. England, as a nation, is not free from the taint of money-lending.[2]

Her action towards her colonies has been very striking from one point of view, as an Athenian or Phœnician perhaps would regard it. Practically, her sons have emigrated to a new country; she has first allowed them to own the land, then encouraged them to mortgage the country to an unlimited extent, while they spend the money as much on gratifying themselves as on enriching their estate. Presently they find themselves in a predicament, in which Australia and New Zealand have been in danger of being placed, *i.e.*, while their resources are crippled, they are burdened with the interest on a tremendous debt.

---

[1] Germany appears to have borrowed from us, as well as receiving the war indemnity from France.

[2] Wilson, writing about 1875, says, "Future generations will cite the conduct of the English in regard to the Turks' constant demand for money [1853-73] as one of the most original examples of folly, and perhaps of crime, that the nineteenth century has to offer."

Note.—Given the sums of money which represent the interest received, less the capital newly invested, and given the total capital abroad at any one time :—If it is permissible to assume that the average rate per cent. does not change rapidly, it is only a somewhat difficult arithmetical problem to find the actual interest and rate per cent. for one year, and hence, working backwards and forwards, to find it for any year. The difficulty of the solution is that individual figures cannot be trusted, but series of years must be taken.

Further, by taking longer intervals, it is (theoretically at any rate) possible to find the total capital invested as well as the interest.

This method has been used, and the results obtained compared with all available estimates, to give the figures used in the text. They are certainly not exact, but it seems improbable that they are much in error.

Note to Revised Edition. — Judging from the information tabulated in the Board of Trade's Memoranda (Cd. 1761, p. 104), the capital held abroad has increased considerably since 1890 ; but as this subject has become a matter of controversy, we do not offer any new estimate.

V.—TRADE IN THE PERIOD, 1870-1892.

1. THE CRISES OF 1873 AND 1883, AND THEIR CAUSES.

THE most marked features of the diagram of imports and exports in 1870-1892 are the two great falls in value; the first, most noticeable in exports, beginning in 1873, and reaching its lowest point in 1878, after which the values increase again till 1882; the second beginning, both in imports and exports, in 1883, while the recovery commences in 1886.

These changes may be due either to diminution of the actual amount of goods exported and imported, or to a reduction of prices of these goods, or to both causes. We shall see subsequently that on the whole the amount rapidly increased, and, therefore, the depression is mainly due to a fall of prices.

Depressions have followed one another in England with a certain regularity at intervals of about ten years through the century. The phenomena attending them are similar. First, an increase in demand and an expectation of high prices have caused an exaggerated output, rash undertakings and credit on too easy terms; then, as the demand is satisfied, prices fall with great rapidity, credit is shaken, and enterprises which had no sound basis fail.

These phenomena are all present in the crisis of

DIAGRAM VI,

showing depressions of trade 1870—1892.

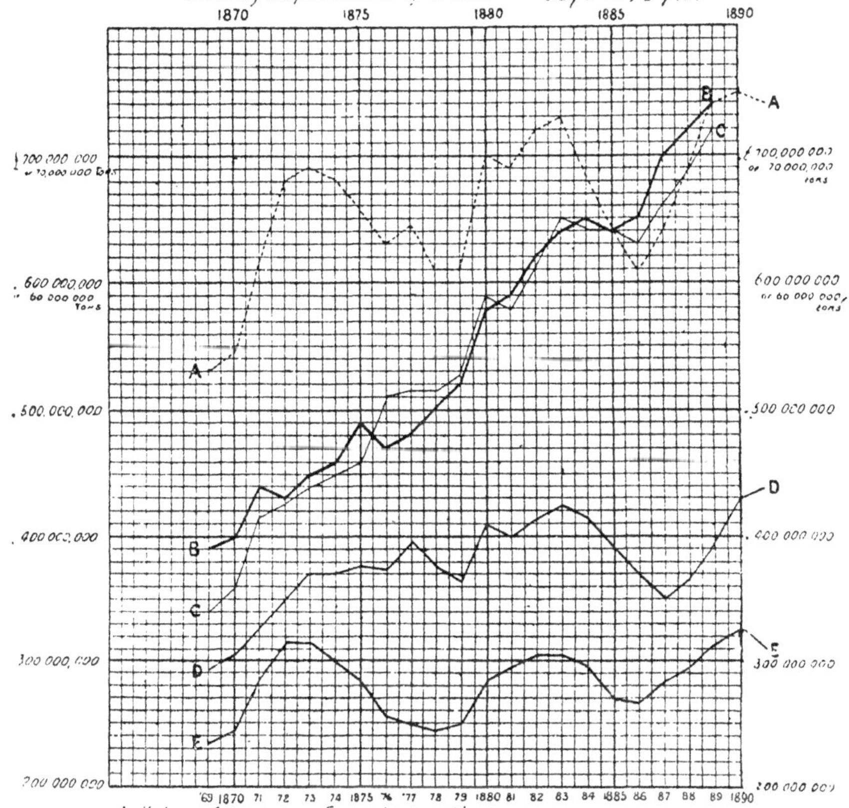

A. Value of Imports & Exports together
B. The same reduced by index numbers to gold values of 1889
C. Shipping entered & cleared to & from Great Britain 1 : 100,000 tons
D. Value of Imports E. Value of Exports, including re exports

1873: "Having its origin in the excessive lock up of capital in the construction of railways, especially in America and Germany, many of which when built had neither population to use them nor traffic to carry; in the wild speculation that followed the German assertion of supremacy on the Continent; in the exaggerated armaments, which withdrew an inordinate amount of labour from productive industry and overweighted the taxpayers of the great European nations, and in over-production in the principal trades in all commercial countries; it was aggravated by a succession of bad harvests in both hemispheres; by famines in the East and in South America; by repudiations by governments and other public debtors; and by the political anxieties which the re-opening of the Eastern Question gave birth to." ("Statist," 1879.)

More generally the cause may be put in this way:—The analogy between the business of an individual and of a nation, though it must not be pushed too far, will illustrate the change of trade before and after 1870. Regarding France, Germany, and the United States as so many individuals engaged in trade, in the years 1820-1850 a great fortune (*i.e.*, mechanical inventions and physical discoveries, aided by Free Trade) fell to England especially, and to the others in part. Naturally elated, and not being able to use his wealth to the full, he (England) lends alike credit, money, and goods to his neighbours, whether their business was sound or shaky, and also to his clerks and sons, who are setting up business on their own account. This process cannot continue; the demand for capital is unnaturally increased, the immense sums lent to and invested by his neighbours cannot at once fructify; inventions, especially tending to accelerate trade, continue to move capital; there are difficulties with employés, whose great need is more work; the natural result is that every little opening is magnified and jumped at, the increasing pace increases risk, and fluctuations are more violent; but there is no real basis for increased trade, and, on the whole, after the first great impulse it remains stationary.

Earlier depressions in the English trade had been felt in America, and as England and the States became more closely connected, any disturbance in one country was at once echoed in the other; but it is most conclusive evidence of the increasing intimacy of international relations, that the depression of 1873 was felt with great severity in "Austria, Germany, Russia, the United States, and the South American countries,"[1] while many other countries were also affected.

The depression was first felt in countries which produced raw materials; borrowing their capital from manufacturing States, and finding the process very profitable, so long as capital was easily obtained, they soon flooded the markets of the old countries with more produce than was required for consumption or manufacture; when the supply of capital was checked, and the demand for raw produce decreased, it was not possible, for instance (even if there had been an

[1] Giffen's "Essays on Finance," p. 109 (First Series), from which source the substance of the following paragraph is also taken.

intimate knowledge of the state of English finance in those remote districts), suddenly to diminish the harvests, to decrease the quantity of corn already sown, to find new employments for the multitude of labourers engaged in agriculture, or pay the interest on, and working expenses of, railways no longer needed. The exploitation of these countries, Austria, the States, South America, and Russia, had been carried too far. Invaluable as their development has proved to the next generation, the capitalists who had supported it, just as the original investors in English railways, suffered great immediate loss.

It is in this direction that we must look for the general cause of the depression; it remains to point out the special events which led to the inflation of 1871 and 1872, and which made 1873 the date of the crisis which was sooner or later inevitable. The Franco-German War, rapid in its course, prolific in wide-reaching results, destroyed wealth in France and Germany alike, for whose re-creation there was room and necessity at its close.[1] Then the war indemnity of £200,000,000 paid to Germany, ultimately out of the hoards of the French peasantry

[1] "The great destruction of capital which is involved in a war, such as that of 1870-1871, naturally stimulates production until the waste of capital is repaired. But when this has been done, and consumption returns to its normal level, the world's capacity of production will naturally be in excess of its ordinary * requirements; and the inevitable result of such a state of things is either a restriction of production, or a reduction in the rate of profit." (Report of Royal Commission on the Depression of Trade, 1886.)

* Perhaps "immediate" would be more correct than "ordinary."

for the most part, caused a great influx of capital into Germany, and an immense demand for English goods especially those connected with railway construction, and produced in Germany such a burst of apparent prosperity that ordinary trade and ordinary methods of business were neglected, and the seeds of commercial disaster sown. The capital overflowed into Austria and Russia, and very soon the world's market was over-stocked, and trade brought to a standstill.

A depression is defined as "a diminution, and in some cases an absence of profit, with a corresponding diminution of employment for the labouring classes." That is to say, though "over-production" under normal conditions is impossible in the long run, yet for a short time the production of large classes of goods may be in excess of any demand at a price which will give profit.

The fall in prices in this depression was the beginning of the long continuous fall, which did not cease till 1895 or 1896. It was aggravated especially by the fact that the inflation was chiefly in the iron and steel trades, where the output cannot be indefinitely increased at once, and where workmen can easily at a time of high prices further increase them by demanding higher wages.

In England the effect was enhanced and prolonged by the increased competition of foreign manufactures, which at that time in Germany and elsewhere were receiving great attention, accompanied by the great reaction against Free Trade, which prevented our manufactures from having a fair chance, except in neutral markets, for continental nations raised their tariffs to keep out our goods, and preserve the home market for their own.

The reaction has been very tardy.[1] Prices have continued to fall, capital having accumulated (which is a sign that the depression is not a serious injury to all classes, as will be seen later), the rate of interest becomes lower and lower,[2] wages rise in England more rapidly than on the Continent, and the lessening profit which the manufacturer can obtain from all these causes has continued to be a cause of grave anxiety.

Another depression began in 1883, but has not so many features of interest as that of 1873. Its' chief characteristics, as summarised in the Majority Report of the Commission on Depression, were—

(a) A very serious falling off in the exchangeable value of the produce of the soil;

(b) An increased production of nearly all other classes of commodities;

(c) A tendency in the supply of commodities to outrun the demand;

(d) A consequent diminution in the profit obtainable by production, and

(e) A similar diminution in the rate of interest on invested capital.

Thus, except that the long, not to say permanent,

[1] This paragraph is as it was written in 1893, since which date the various factors have changed.

[2] So far as the manufacturer borrows capital this is, of course, a benefit to him; but profits on fixed capital fall when interest on new capital is small.

depression in English agriculture was a comparatively new and effective factor in the difficulties of trade, this depression does not differ from previous ones. It makes prominent, however, some of the chief features of our modern trade, which will be discussed later, *viz.*, the increasing severity of competition both in production and manufacture of raw materials, the diminishing profits which capital can secure, and the gradual displacement of trades, which always brings bitter complaints from those who are injured by it.

2. THE CONSTRUCTION OF RAILWAYS, AND THE EFFECT OF INCREASED FACILITIES OF TRANSPORT.

"It is not too much to say that in the years 1869-1872 the foreign railways, and other undertakings launched, were such as there were not materials in the markets of the whole world to carry through without an enhancement of values that should not only render the undertakings themselves hopeless, but seriously cripple much well-established trade." (*Encyclopædia Britannica.*)

From this statement we further see the great influence that railway construction had on the depression of trade; and it will be well to give a brief review of the history of railways from their first beginning, in order to be able to judge more clearly their effect on industrial movements.

As we have seen,[1] England took the lead in Europe, and had developed her system before 1850, having constructed 6,600 miles, or about one-third of her

[1] IV. 1 *supra.*

present total, at that date. France began railway building in 1841, Italy in 1850, other European countries in the sixth decade of the century, causing an increase of iron and steel exports from England from £8,000,000 in 1850 to £24,000,000 in 1860.[1]

The total numbers of the miles in use at the following dates were—[2]

	1840	1850	1860	1870	1880	1890
United Kingdom.	800	6,600	10,400	15,500	17,900	19,800
The Continent of Europe, . .	800	7,800	21,400	47,800	83,800	110,200
United States, .	2,800	9,000	30,600	53,400	93,600	156,000
India, . . .	...	...	800	4,800	9,300	16,000
Australia, . .	...	...	200	1,200	5,400	10,100
The rest of the World, . .	...	...	2,800	5,500	18,400	42,200
Total, . .	4,500	23,500	66,200	128,200	228,400	354,300

Between 1860 and 1880 railways on the Continent increased four-fold, and in the United States three-fold. Most of these lines were projected between 1869 and 1872; the figures of our exports of steel and iron being—

1868	2,042,000 tons,	£17,634,000
1872	3,383,000 ,,	35,996,000
1876	2,224,000 ,,	20,737,000,

while our increased exports to Germany and the United States show their destination.

[1] For this and other details, *vide* line D in Diagram vii.

[2] Mulhall's "Dictionary of Statistics."

After each of the great railway booms of the century, for instance in England about 1847, in America before 1857 and 1873, in India in 1878, and on the Continent in 1873, the collapse has been very violent for the materials are bought at exaggerated prices; the weekly wage during construction is enormous; no return is obtained till the whole scheme, whose carrying out probably lasts many years, is complete; and in 1870 this return was further delayed by a new cause.

Until this date, railways had chiefly been constructed in order to facilitate intercourse along old channels, to bring into closer connection the great manufacturing centres with each other and with the great markets; but now we arrive at a new era of railway building, already foreshadowed in the United States, when the great accumulation of capital in England and the accession of wealth to Germany were ready to be used for developing new countries. Railways are often built in order to create a traffic, and sometimes a new industry and even a population; this has frequently been the case in America, is often the case in suburban districts in England, and was especially so in lines projected at this time; that is to say, lines were extended into partially populated and partially cultivated districts, whose population had no acquaintance with foreign trade, no surplus to export, no wish to travel. After the railways were completed, all this was gradually changed. Cultivation increased, and so did population; the old resources of the land were developed, more than was necessary for local consumption was produced; mineral and other natural wealth, hitherto profitless, was ready for export; the traffic grew, and the existence of the railways was ultimately justified.[1]

But, in the interval, the immense capital locked up had no return, labour was merely drawn from productive industries, ordinary trades suffered, capital and enterprise being diverted from them, and thus the railway boom of 1869-1872 was the most effective cause of the long depression which followed. Gradually the capital locked up in these and other enterprises began to yield profit, trade returned to its normal condition, and the end of the depression was marked by further railway construction in the States, which gave a stimulus to our iron and steel trade in 1880. Since that date, vast as has been the expansion of the railway system of the United States, its influence on English trade has been neutralised by the growing production of steel in America.

The railway boom of 1870 did not extend to India. The figures of Indian railways show a rapid extension from 1860 to 1863, a comparatively regular increase till 1879, and from then till 1891 a more rapid growth of some 800 miles per annum.

As has already been indicated, the extension of railways has always had a double influence on English trade; first, during the long period in which England was the sole manufactory of iron and steel

[1] This is not inconsistent with the fact that there was already (in 1873) an excess of raw materials from new countries. Both the lines then in use, and those only in construction, were, after no long interval, fully employed owing to the rapid growth of trade and population.

on a large scale, and when these manufactures occupied almost the first place in our industrial system, every new railway, projected in any country, had an immediate effect on the volume and value of our exports; secondly, the very existence of each new profitable railway is a proof that another method has been found of making transport from new sources possible or of reducing existing freights, and it is the extension of railways over the world which has produced that cheapness and facility of transport, without which foreign trade could hardly exist.

Whether England is losing her hold on the steel trade or no, that trade has had permanent effects on her industrial position. With her natural advantages of large coal and iron districts adjoining each other, with the stamina, endurance, and energy of English workmen, and with the continual stimulus of renewed demands and consequent new inventions, her production, by its excellent quality, helped to establish her commercial reputation, and by its quantity and value was very instrumental in giving her the financial advantage, which she still possesses, of having large sums due to her from other nations. [See Note 6, p. 152.]

In all Mr. Brassey's experience in railway contracting from 1840-1870, when tenders for bridges, locomotives, or steel were issued to all nations, it was always English firms who supplied the greater part, generally the whole, of the goods for delivery in Europe, India, or Australia. Recently, as is well known, owing to the partial exhaustion of English mines and their development in other countries, our supremacy in this direction has diminished; but our iron and steel are still of as great importance as of old for the building of iron ships. When the opening of the Suez Canal necessitated a new class of steamers, with a rapid realisation of the new qualities needed, most creditable to English merchants, a large fleet of iron steamships was built with great rapidity; a final blow was thus given to shipbuilding in America, already nearly destroyed by suicidal tariffs on wood, and England obtained the business of the canal and made secure the supremacy of her merchant navy.

The Clyde not only supplied her own trade with steamers, but in all countries, though tenders for building were open to the whole world, it was always an English firm who obtained the contract. In 1870 all the steamers of the British-Indian fleet, all of the North German Lloyd's, 60 per cent. of the Austrian Lloyd's, and eight-ninths of the Azizieh Egyptian line, were of British construction. Our supremacy in this respect continues till the present date, and in the five years, 1899-1903, vessels to the extent of nearly 900,000 tons burden were built in the United Kingdom for foreigners.

The evidence of the reduction of freights, so far as any is needed, is to be found by merely considering the sources of our raw materials.

There is a permanent competition between railways and canals and navigable rivers; in the one case rapidity and convenience, and in the other economy, are to be found. The canal system of England would have been further developed but for the sudden mania for railways which occurred while canals were still being connected and completed. Importation of wheat by the great water-ways of Southern Russia is older than the extension of railways. Now freights by water have diminished, railways have brought the interior of India, North Russia, Canada, and the vast tracts of the United States into competition with the older maritime sources of our grain supply. No keener, more lasting, or more extensive competition can be imagined. Differences of soil, of climate, of methods of cultivation, of habits of life, all have their influence on the price of the grain before it is placed on the railway, canal, or sea; but to such perfection have methods of transport been brought, that Australia, Canada, Germany, and Essex all place wheat at London at the same price; and not only is it possible to bring corn these vast distances at a remunerative price, but with the reduction of freights this price continually falls.

Gazette Price of Wheat and Meal (Average for 10 Years).			Reduced by[1] Index Nos.	Average Imports (Millions of cwts.)
1831-40	56s. 11d.	per quarter.	59s. 6d.	—
1841-50	53s. 4d.	,,	62s. 2d.	—
1851-60	54s. 7d.	,,	57s. 4d.	28
1861-70	51s. 1d.	,,	51s. 3d.	35
1871-80	51s. 1d.	,,	53s. 3d.	56
1881-90	35s. 9½d.	,,	47s. 9d.	77
1891-1900	28s. 3d.	,,	42s. 7d.	97

In spite of these gradually falling prices, it has been possible to send us continually increasing stores of grain, and when we find that in 1868 it cost 65s. to send a ton of wheat from Chicago to Liverpool, while

[1] See Note on p. 96.

in 1884 it cost 24s., and has since been further reduced, there is no room for surprise at this increase.

A glance at the published figures[1] of imported grain shows another result. Nothing can be more variable than the figures for different countries year by year, while the totals for all show a not irregular increase. We are no longer dependent on the harvest at home or in any one district for cheapness and plenty. Before our supply can run short, there must be a drought in both hemispheres, and in the Southern and Northern summers. It was not the absence of grain in the world that caused the recent famine in Russia, it was the absence of means of transport to the suffering districts.

The same phenomenon is seen, but to a less degree, in the supply of cotton. The totals progress regularly, the imports from the United States are not irregular, but the supplies from other countries fluctuate violently. [See Note 4, p. 151.]

It is not necessary to multiply instances of the reductions of freight. The effect has been the same on other raw materials as on wheat, and the reductions on manufactures have been as great as on raw materials.

The cotton trade will, however, supply interesting evidence on this point.

The freights for cotton were (in pence per lb.)—

In 1872.	In 1888.	
1.190	.560	Bombay to Lancashire : cotton.
.985	.500	Lancashire to Bombay : yarn.
2.175	1.060	Import of cotton and export of yarn from and to India.
	.70	Lancashire to Japan or China.
	.26	Bombay to Japan or China.

[1] *Vide* Statistical Abstracts.

Thus since 1872 freights have diminished by one-half; and in 1888 cotton could be brought from India to England and sent when manufactured to Japan at the total cost of 1¼d. per lb., so that the differences of situation only makes the following differences in price for the same quality of yarn :—

Selling in India.	In China or Japan.
Indian spinner, 7½d.[1]	7¾d.
English spinner, 8¼d.[2]	8½d.

At the same time, on heavier goods, such as coal and machinery, the freights were still so heavy that coal in Bombay was three times the English price, while machinery was 25 per cent. dearer in India than in England; such exports, however, would have been almost impossible before the improvement of means of transport.

Great as the reduction of freights has been, it has hardly been so great as the quickening of transport and communication.

Instead of twelve miles an hour for passengers and four miles an hour for goods, forty miles is considered slow for the first, while for inland traffic, time of transport is so diminished as no longer to be an important item.

By sea, goods are no longer at the mercy of the weather, nor need they be sent only at calm seasons, or to obtain certain winds.

It was thought incredible, in 1872, that the journey

[1] Raw cotton, 5d.; cost of manufacturing, 2½d.—total, 7½d.

[2] Raw cotton in India, 5d.; transport to England, ½d.; manufacturing, 2¼d.; transport to India, ½d.—total, 8¼d.

from England to Hong-Kong could be made in thirty-six days, though steamers were already aiming at their present perfection: now it has been accomplished in twenty-four days, and there is no reason to think further reductions improbable. Similarly the journey from New York to London was reduced from nine days in 1872 to six days in 1893.

These are the reductions as steamers tend towards their limit of speed, and are as nothing to the reduction from the old sailing times. Thirty-five days to Australia and twenty-two to Calcutta are the times that replace the three or four months required before railways, or steamers, or the Suez Canal were known.

But the greatest quickening has, of course, been in communication. By the telegraph an answer can be obtained in, at most, a few hours, instead of in six months. Large accumulations of goods are at once rendered unnecessary, for they can be placed on ship in Australia on the day following the order in England; London need no longer be the depôt for Eastern produce; the middleman is displaced, and the carrying out of bargains economised.

Again, much of the waste of wrongly anticipating a future demand is avoided. The state of the market at Manchester is known at once in Bombay and in America, and exactly the right quantity and quality of goods can be sent.

To sum up, all the mechanical inventions, the growth of enterprise, and the freedom of trade, would have been of slight avail, till railways made new countries accessible, steamers brought them close together, and the telegraph practically annihilated time.

1905.—Note to p. 92. This column is of great importance in view of recent statements that the Repeal of the Corn Laws did not reduce the price of wheat.

3. DIGRESSION ON SILVER AND ITS HISTORY (1870-1893).

At present Great Britain and many of her dependencies use gold as legal tender in payment for all debts, and silver only to a small amount.

France, Italy, and some other European countries use gold chiefly, but keep a limited amount of silver in circulation.

In China, India,[1] other Eastern countries, Mexico, and Spanish America, silver only is current.

Till 1870, few inconveniences arose out of this difference of standard. The price of silver in European countries varied very little; there was no difficulty in selling rupees in Europe, or buying them in India at a constant rate.

But changes began to occur in about 1870. The output of American silver mines was greatly increased, the price of silver began to fall, and European countries, which had been in the habit of accepting any quantity of silver at a fixed rate and coining it free, now found that they were buying above the market rate, and that gold was being driven out of ordinary circulation, for it was used for

[1] See pp. 101, 102 for the alterations made in 1893.

buying silver, and selling it at a premium to the Government.

Consequently, Germany, the Latin Union, and Holland limited their silver coinage, and Germany melted down great quantities of her silver coins. Every other European country was obliged to follow their example; the increased American supply, further increased by this melting down of coins, met with a reduced demand, and the price of silver fell greatly.

This injured the silver party in the United States; and under their influence in 1878 their market was extended, and the price raised, by an act compelling the purchase by the States Treasury of silver to the amount of $2,000,000 monthly; vendors of silver obtained certificates for the amount sold, which, being legal tender for certain purposes, practically regulated the currency. Meanwhile five-sixths of this silver merely filled the Treasury vaults.

The result was continual agitation among political parties in America, repeated "corners" in silver, and the most violent fluctuations in the price of silver, felt all over the world. [See Note 8, p. 155.]

We have to trace the effects on our trade of these two phenomena — short fluctuations, and a long continuous fall in the price of silver.

The first merely affects the actual transaction of business between gold- and silver-using countries. When a purchase is made in England of goods to be bought in India, the price in gold in England necessarily varies with the price in silver in India; the amount in gold agreed to be paid must be that which will exchange in India for the silver necessary to buy the goods there. If the exchange ratio of silver for gold is constantly changing, and may change considerably between the beginning and completion of the purchase, the risks and uncertainties of trade are indefinitely increased, and a sudden change in the exchange ratio has often brought business temporarily to a standstill.

The same difficulty is felt in arranging the revenue; the estimate is based on the expected exchange value of the rupee which it is impossible to foretell; if the value diminishes there is a deficit, while if it increases, taxation has been unnecessarily increased, which in India is a great evil.

The second effect is more important and far-reaching. The price of silver has fallen in just the same way, and very nearly at the same rate, as the prices of other commodities. That is to say, while in countries having a gold standard there has been a fall of prices amounting to 30 per cent. in twenty years, in silver-using countries at the same time prices have changed less rapidly, for "silver prices are, it is said, less subject to alteration, through causes affecting the currency, than gold prices. The immense volume of silver in Eastern countries, the conservative habits of the people, the absence of banking facilities and other commercial facilities, all contribute to this result:"[1] that is, there is a natural tendency for prices measured in silver to remain stationary in the East; and the equal increase of silver and

[1] Gold and Silver Commission, 1887. But see article by Mr. Morison, *Stat. Journal*, 1902, p. 513.

commodities all over the world has emphasised this tendency.

Now, wages in Europe, ultimately,[1] are adjusted to changes in prices, falling when prices are low and rising when they are high; but there is a very strong tendency for the effect on wages to linger behind the change in prices: when prices rise, wages often rise less, as was the case in factories in 1812, and when prices fall, workmen often find it possible to continue to obtain wages at the old rate: in fact, it is at the time of falling prices that it is most easy for real incomes (*i.e.*, incomes as measured by purchasing power) to increase; this was the case between 1815 and 1843, and since 1870 the increase of money wages has been greatly enhanced by the fall of prices.

The result is that in England and the rest of Europe, prices measured on a gold basis have fallen, but wages have not. In India, prices and wages have not changed their relation so much.

Thus, an Indian manufacturer continues to obtain workmen and Indian materials at the same rate, while an English manufacturer, paying the same wages in gold, is paying more in real value; and the prices measured in gold at which he can sell profitably will not fall.

For instance, if an Indian manufacturer paid twenty rupees for work done in 1872, and sold for twenty-five rupees, thus making 25 per cent. profit, the same figures will represent the corresponding transaction in 1892.

But reckoned in gold, in 1872, at 2s. the rupee, he

[1] In the absence of causes of permanent increase or decrease.

paid £2 and sold for £2 10s.; while in 1892, at 1s. 6d. the rupee, he paid £1 10s. and sold for £1 17s. 6d.

The European manufacturer meanwhile has to pay the same gold price for work done in 1892 and 1872; thus, when Indian and English goods compete in a neutral market, the change in exchange value gives India a distinct advantage.

The fall of 1d. in the exchange value of the rupee gives the Indian spinner an advantage[1] of about $\frac{1}{10}$d. per lb. of cotton.[2] But we shall presently[3] see that it is not merely this cause that is enabling him to compete with the Manchester manufacturer. Just the same has occurred with regard to Indian wheat: the Indian grower obtains his seed, land, and labour at the old silver prices, whereas the English grower pays (apart from other disturbing causes) the old gold prices; it is said that when the rupee falls 1d., India can export wheat to us at a reduction of 1s. 6d. per quarter measured in our money; but this is not the only cause that regulates the importation of Indian wheat.

It should be clearly understood that the advantage comes from this fact: reckoned in purchasing power, wages of English labour have become greater, but wages of Indian labour have not.

It must be observed, however, that the fall is not all gain to India. Debts contracted with gold countries must be paid in gold; that is, in an increased number of rupees. Wages in any way dependent on

[1] Report of Manchester Cotton Spinning Inquiry.

[2] Cotton yarn costs about 2½d. per lb. to spin.

[3] *Vide* VI. 1 *infra*.

gold must be increased in rupees. In the case of the Indian Civil Service and the Army, just and bitter complaints are made of the effects of the fall. Salaries are paid in silver, but a large part of them are spent in England or on English goods, in which case, now that fifteen rupees are needed to obtain a sovereign, instead of ten, as was the case when the salaries were arranged, Indian salaries lose one-third of their value.

Remembering, however, that prices as a whole have fallen, another way of putting the same thing is this:

Indian officers and civil servants have not benefited by the general fall in prices, whereas their compeers in the Home Service have.

Hong-Kong and all settlements where silver is the currency have suffered in just the same way. Profits, interest, and capital, when realised, must be transmitted home at a lower value and consequent loss.

It is not within our scope to discuss bi-metallism—that is, the theory that by universal agreement the ratio between gold and silver can be fixed and kept constant—as a remedy for this confusion. The objections to its adoption are chiefly based on the apparent impossibility of coming to an agreement, and the alleged impossibility of preserving the fixed ratio without immense loss; it is also contended that bi-metallism would not have the remedial effects that its advocates suppose.

An attempt is now[1] being made by the Indian Government to introduce a gold currency into India;

[1] July, 1893.

gold has been made the standard of the country. Silver is only to be coined at 1s. 4d. the rupee (fifteen rupees to the pound sterling); rupees are still legal tender, and internal trade will not be affected; but it is hoped that a reserve of gold will be accumulated from the supply known to be hoarded in India, and that as far as India is concerned the rupee will be kept at a stationary exchange value, to which all transactions can be adjusted. [See Note 8, p. 155.]

4. THE STEADY INCREASE OF VOLUME OF IMPORTS AND EXPORTS, AND THE PROPORTION PER HEAD OF THE POPULATION.

The effects of the depression which began in 1873 must not be exaggerated. In the figures of total imports and exports, as published, it is very striking; but when we allow for the general and continuous fall in prices, which took place concurrently with the decreased value of imports, we find that the amount (measured in goods, not in money) of foreign trade transacted has continually increased.[1]

The depression affected capitalists and their profits, shook credit, checked for many years the outflow of capital abroad, and made employment uncertain for the small proportion of employés and workmen who are dependent on those trades which fluctuate in sympathy with foreign disturbance; but the amount of cotton imported did not diminish, wool imports increased steadily, while our foreign supply of wheat grew faster than the population.

[1] *Vide* Diagram vi.

When reduced by the index numbers to the value of 1871, which is the fair way to make comparisons for a series of years, the import and export figures are these:—

Year.	Total Imports and Exports. Millions of £.	The same reduced to Gold Values of 1871. Total.	Per head of Population.
1870	547	570	18
1873	682	613	19
1876	631	664	20
1879	611	736	21·5
1882	719	856	24·5
1885	642	891	25
1888	685	980	26·5
1890	748	1,070	28
1895	703	1,130	29

The shipping figures show a similar increase:—

Year.	Tonnage of Vessels Entered and Cleared at Ports in United Kingdom.	Per Head of Population.
1870	36 million	17
1873	44 ,,	21
1876	50 ,,	23
1879	52 ,,	23
1882	61 ,,	26
1885	64 ,,	26
1888	68 ,,	27
1890	74 ,,	30
1895	80 ,,	31

(Per head figures: of $\frac{1}{15}$ of a ton.)

The close resemblance of the figures in the two right-hand columns is very striking, considering that they are obtained from totally different sources by different methods.[1] They appear to show that the

[1] See *Econ. Journal*, 1897, p. 277, and 1903, p. 629. The correspondence is not close between 1895 and 1902.

H

shipping statistics are the best index of the volume (as opposed to the nominal value) of foreign trade. It is to this volume that we must look when we are considering the benefits of our trade to the consumer. The consumer does not inquire whether trade is profitable, or brisk, or languishing. He may be interested in that when he is considering his income; but in making his purchase his only concern is what proportion the price bears to his means.

In order to estimate practically the proportion of each person's income which is used for purchases of foreign goods, and the changes of that proportion, many data are necessary. First, the total value of imports; secondly, the proportion of raw materials to goods for consumption; and thirdly, the population at every date, whence the value per head, both of raw and other goods, is found. These figures can be estimated approximately. This value must next be reduced by index numbers to some standard year, and we then have found the quantity of goods imported for each person. This quantity has continually increased from 1840 till the present date. It increased rapidly from 1855 till 1872; was checked, but hardly diminished, before the commencement of the depression in values; and from 1876 onwards has, notwithstanding fluctuations and depressions in values, steadily grown. [This is still the case, 1905.]

We have thus very definite evidence that these depressions do not affect the consumer to his disadvantage; goods are offered, rather, at reduced prices, and with his former expenditure he obtains more of them. Benefiting the consumer at the expense of the producer has in the mass the paradoxical effect of benefiting the nation at its own expense, for consumers are in most cases also producers; but by a depression certain classes of incomes are greatly diminished, while at the same time the spending power of all incomes is slightly increased.

It does not follow that depressions are good for commerce or for the production of wealth. A regular progress of trade would give all the advantages which appear to come from a depression, without the dislocation of trade and the loss to individuals.

There are still other data necessary before an accurate estimate of the growing importance of foreign trade is possible. We must know the total expenditure before we know the proportion spent on foreign goods, as we must know the total amount of goods produced before we can tell what proportion of our energy is spent in producing goods for export. Unfortunately, it is not possible to obtain these facts; statistical knowledge is not far enough advanced.

As far as is known, the facts in 1904 are something like the following:—The total income of the country is now £1,800,000,000 per annum, or about £42 per head. The total expenditure is not known, but perhaps £6 per head (some £250,000,000 for the country) is saved, while £36 is spent. Of this, £5 goes for imported food, £3 for imported manufactures, and £3 for raw materials, of which part is used for manufactures for home consumption.

As regards real incomes — that is, wages or salaries reckoned by their purchasing power—their improvement has, but for very short periods, been continuous since 1775.

From 1775 to 1815 prices rose, but incomes rose still more.
From 1820 to 1851 prices fell 35 per cent., while incomes remained nearly steady.
From 1851 to 1873 prices rose 50 per cent., but incomes rose 60 per cent.
From 1873 to 1895 prices fell 45 per cent., while incomes fell, but rose again to the 1873 level.
From 1895 to 1901 prices rose 12 per cent., but incomes rose 15 per cent.

Combining these and similar figures, we have—

AVERAGE INCOME CORRECTED BY WHOLESALE INDEX NUMBERS, AND EXPRESSED AS PERCENTAGE OF THE HEIGHT IN 1901.

1820	1851	1871	1873	1881	1891	1895	1901
35	45	54	55	67	84	98	100

These figures must not be used indiscriminately. They merely state that with the average income there could be obtained in 1901 three times as much of many of the commodities commonly consumed, directly or indirectly, as could be obtained with the average income in 1820; and similarly for other years. But many important items of expenditure or cost are not taken into account; *e.g.*, rent, the value of land, the difference between wholesale and retail prices, the price of personal services, rendered directly or by officials. The inclusion of these would probably diminish the rate of increase.

We can from the above figures and the statistics

of Imports and Exports obtain the following rough table:—

CORRECTING GOLD VALUES BY INDEX NUMBERS, SO AS TO OBTAIN A CONSTANT STANDARD, *viz.*: VALUE OF GOLD IN 1901.

		Spent on Imports.	
	Average Income.	Average Sum.	Percentage of Total.
1820 ...	£15	£0·8	6
1851 ...	19	3·3	17
1871 ...	23	5·3	22
1881 ...	28	7·0	25
1891 ...	35	9·0	26
1902 ...	42	10·8	26

We thus see that the quantity of imports for each person has steadily increased; but that the fraction of real income spent on imports has increased little since 1871.

VI.—ENGLAND'S PRESENT POSITION.

1. THE PRESENT POSITION OF ENGLAND'S GREAT TRADES.

WE have now reviewed briefly the most important events which have affected our foreign trade during the nineteenth century, and the most striking features of its growth, and are in a position to estimate the relative importance of her greatest industries, and to point out the circumstances which influence her hold on them.

It may be convenient to adopt the divisions used by the Labour Commission, *viz.*:—

1. Minerals and hardware.
2. Textiles.
3. Transport.

1. Both the coal and iron trades are now in a state of transition. [See Notes 6 and 7, pp. 152-4.]

In 1840 coal formed only 1·1 per cent. in value of our total exports; this proportion has steadily increased, and in 1891 had reached more than 8 per cent. of our exports of home produce; about one-tenth of this is, however, exported for use by our own steamers. Coal is therefore an important part of our trade, but it is evident that its importance cannot extend through more than one or two generations

DIAGRAM VII,

showing the character of Exports, 1849 - 1904.

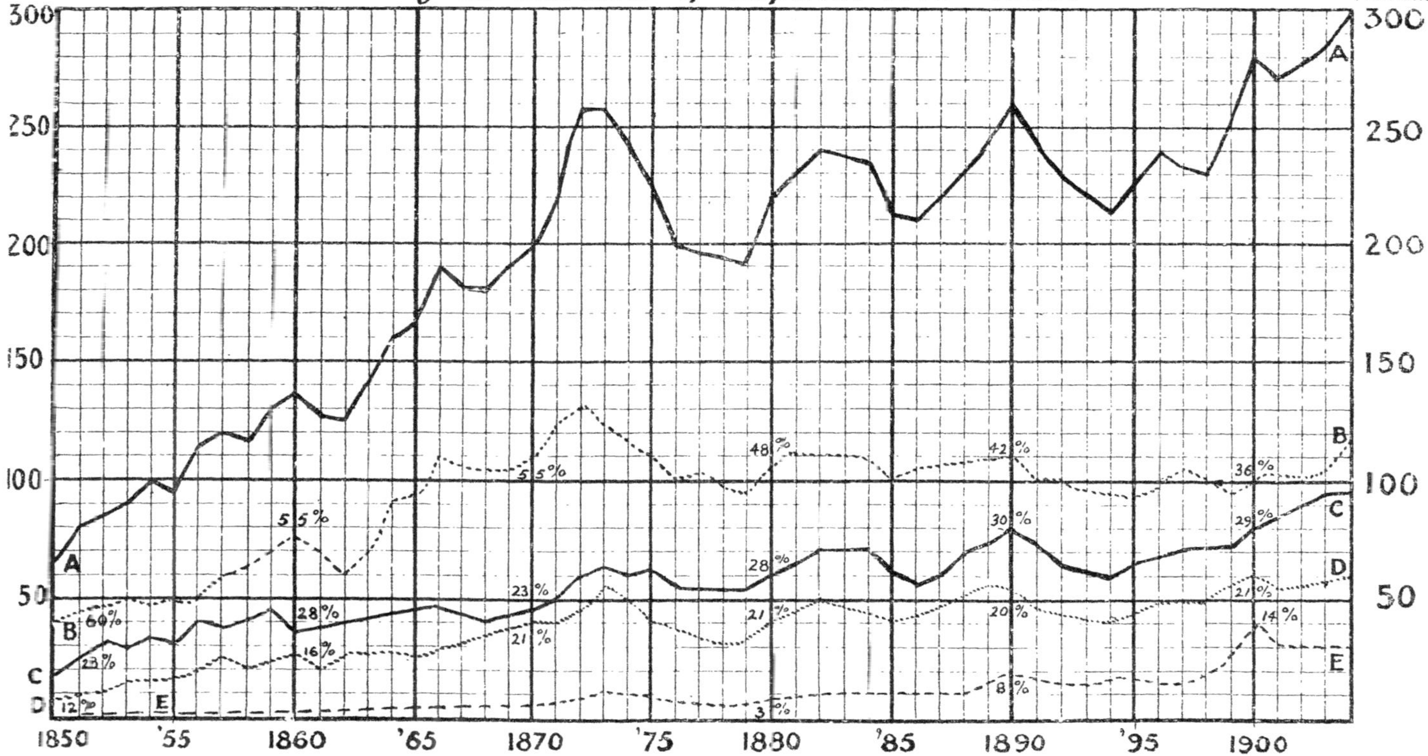

A. Declared total value of Exports of British and Irish Produce.
B. " " " of Textiles.
C. " " " other than B, D and E.
D. " " " of Iron and Steel and Manufactures thereof, Machinery, Cutlery, Hardware, &c.

under the most favourable estimate of our coal resources, unless totally new fields are discovered. It seems probable that after a short time the increasing depth from which coal must be obtained will add to its cost and diminish its production, that a larger proportion will be needed for the home demand, which, considering the cost of transport and the probable development of foreign supplies, will be stronger than the foreign demand, and that the first effect of increased difficulty in raising coal will be felt in our foreign trade.

After the experience of this century, however, with its many startling and unforeseen developments, it is unsafe to lay stress on any cause which may produce no effect for twenty or thirty years. This caution is especially needed in the face of the pessimistic cries that we must lose our trade entirely when our coal verges towards exhaustion; for besides the fact that coal is only one of the important factors of our commercial supremacy, we may reasonably expect that the increasing stimulus which the rising price would supply will produce inventions towards economy in its mining and use, and that before the conclusion of the time allowed by our prophets for the exhaustion of coal, other motive powers—water, electricity, gas, or oil may be brought into practical utility.

Steel and iron have in the same way as coal had much to do with establishing our pre-eminence commercially, and have had a continuous and changing effect on our foreign trade relations.

It was by these exports that we became the

creditors of the world, during the two eras of foreign railway construction, 1853-57 and 1870-73.

Looking at the proportion that the value of iron and steel exported bears to the total value of exports of home produce, we find that it was about 3 per cent. in 1840, that it rose to a maximum of 8·6 per cent. in 1854, fell to 5·3 per cent. in 1866, rose again to 9·8 per cent. in 1873, returning to 5 per cent. in 1884-6. The *quantities* exported would, of course, give totally different figures, for it is notorious that iron and steel fluctuate in price violently as the demand rises and falls. The output cannot be increased or diminished indefinitely at short notice, and rising prices have frequently been further raised by strikes and combinations of workmen.

The proportion of our production of steel and iron to that of the world is diminishing. [See Note 6, p. 152.]

The production of pig-iron and steel has been—

(In Thousands of Tons.)

	1860.	1870.	1880.	1885.	1889.
England, . .	3,830	5,960	7,750	7,420	8,250
United States, .	820	1,670	3,840	4,050	7,600
Other countries, .	2,530	4,280	6,550	7,630	9,310
Total, .	7,180	11,910	18,140	19,100	25,160[1]

The necessity for importing ores for subsidiary processes and the gradual exhaustion of our own mines, together with the development of foreign mines, naturally account for this. Since one of our great advantages in this manufacture is the nearness of our

[1] Mulhall's "Dictionary of Statistics."

coal to our iron and to the sea, it will be seen that any rise in the price of coal must have a great effect in handicapping us in the manufacture of iron and steel.

It is not unlikely that the minerals, which have helped so much to give us the supremacy which we have hitherto enjoyed, will, by the natural process of exhaustion of old mines and development of new, a process which no laws or organisation can possibly stop, become in the not distant future a less important branch of our trade. But there is no reason to think that English energy, denied outlet in this direction, will therefore be unused; we have other manufactures, continually growing in number, which may well dwarf our exports of coal and iron (amounting as they do to less than 22 per cent. of our whole exports); we are not dependent on any one branch of trade.

Supposing all this trade lost in twenty-two years, a very improbable event, it would only mean the annual loss or transfer of 1 per cent. of that fraction of our whole capital and labour which is employed in foreign trade, a less calamity than a bad harvest early in the century or a destructive war now. Even when we add to this the possible increased cost in general manufacturing, not incurred by our foreign rivals (no very great increase, for in the cotton trade coal only accounts for one-fiftieth part of the whole cost of manufacture), there is no great cause for alarm; in thus estimating future losses, we are endeavouring to forecast the future of trade in a way which the experience derived from the changes of this century should show us to be unwise.

The moral is that every effort should be made to

widen the basis of our trade, and this we shall shortly see is continually being done.

2. The textile manufactures bring more distinctly before us the effect of other nations undertaking for themselves what hitherto has been done for them by us. [See Notes 4 and 5, pp. 151, 152.]

The causes that have made England the seat of the cotton manufacture are not quite as obvious as those which give us coal and steel. The factors that would naturally seem of importance are nearness to the raw material, to coal and to supplies of machinery, and the command of organised and skilled labour. Taking these in order :—The carriage of cotton has been so wonderfully reduced that, as we have seen, distance from the supply makes little difference. Coal is not a large item in the expense of manufacturing; our supply has been better than that of competing nations, but we appear to be losing this advantage. We have long enjoyed complete command of the best machinery; but other nations are acquiring the necessary knowledge and skill to supply themselves. Our power rests on the immense capital permanently invested, on the long, continuous training of workmen and masters in skill and management, on our damp climate, which aids the process, and on our long-established supremacy.

Our possession of the cotton and transport trades will at first sight puzzle future students; but it is not difficult to trace the events which gave us the former. When America had her crop to export, and wished to obtain manufactures in return, we were (and till long afterwards) supreme in manufacturing; wool gave us cotton; cotton gave us factories; factories gave foreign trade; foreign trade brought us more cotton. The question as to how long we shall keep command of the cotton trade is not so easy to answer, nor is it essential to answer it. It is not likely that we shall lose it suddenly, for it would necessarily take years of accumulation before the necessary plant could be ready elsewhere. If the course of trade does prove that other countries can be more cheaply supplied by themselves than by us, then we must gradually divert our energy to trades that will pay, or to producing at home those things which we now obtain in exchange for cotton goods.

What has happened is that our exports of cotton have (allowing for fluctuations) increased in quantity, remained stationary in value, and diminished in proportion to our whole exports; and that other countries have begun to manufacture for themselves, to supply their own increasing wants, and have exported to other markets quantities which are small, except in the case of exports from the United States to China, and Central and South America, and from France to Algeria and Indo-China.

The following are the figures of our trade:—

EXPORTS OF COTTON YARN AND MANUFACTURES.

Year.	Piece Goods.	Yarn & Thread.	Value of total Cotton Exports.	Percentage of whole exports of British and Irish Produce.
1861	2,563 million yds.	183 million lbs.	£46,872,489	37
1870	3,266 ,,	193 ,,	£71,416,345	35
1880	4,495 ,,	228 ,,	£75,564,056	34
1890	5,124 ,,	276 ,,	£74,730,749	28

The Indian manufacture is a very important factor in the immediate future of this trade. India has produced and worked up cotton for ages, but factories, in the present sense of the word, were not started till after the time of the American Civil War. These factories have the obvious advantage of saving the double transport of cotton and yarn. It was reckoned from the state of the trade in 1888[1] that the Indian had in 1872 an advantage of $1\frac{1}{2}$d. a lb. over the Lancashire spinner from this cause.

He was further helped by a duty on imported yarn, and after some reverses was able to obtain a firm hold on first the Indian and then the Chinese and Eastern market. He is hindered by having to import coals and machinery, though the development of Indian coalfields will probably soon cheapen his supply; while the English spinner has been benefited by the great reduction of freights already mentioned, by which the Indian advantage is reduced by $1\frac{1}{10}$d. per lb.[2] Again, he has been helped by the fall in exchange,[3] which it is reckoned has yielded a gain of ^{3} d. per lb., while the rupee fell from 2s. to 1s. 7d., and an increased gain on its further fall. Now that the exchange value of the rupee has been fixed, he will retain, but not increase, this advantage in India, while for China and the East it may continue to vary.

The continual fluctuations of the exchange have also been a handicap on Lancashire, for when the rupee suddenly falls 1d., no immediate difference is

[1] The following figures are taken from the "Manchester Cotton Spinning Inquiry."

[2] *Vide* p. 92 *supra.* [3] *Vide* V. 3 *supra.*

felt by silver-using manufacturers. They can sell without loss at the old price; but the Lancastrian, having all his expenses measured in gold, must suffer the whole loss, or, as more often happens, postpone his sale till matters have got adjusted. Raw cotton immediately rises to the English price for all concerned; coal and other materials imported into India have soon their effect in raising their fraction of the cost of manufacturing to the gold value; so that after a short time the Indian advantage is reduced to the small fraction due to wages (less than $\frac{1}{10}$d. per lb. for each fall of 1d.), and the English business can be carried on.

The result is that at present in the actual manufacturing and placing in the market, the Indian spinner has a pull over his English rival of about $\frac{3}{4}$d. per lb. in Japan, China, and Hong-Kong, and $\frac{7}{8}$d. in India,[1] and is not hindered by fluctuations in exchange.

Under these circumstances, the thing to be wondered at is that India has not gained more of our trade. That she has obtained a great part of the cotton trade with the East is shown by the following table:—

EXPORTATIONS OF COTTON YARNS TO CHINA, HONG-KONG, AND JAPAN.

	From India.	From England.
1876	8 million lbs.	29 million lbs.
1880	26 ,,	46 ,,
1884	65 ,,	38 ,,
1887	113 ,,	35 ,,
1890[2]	... ,,	38 ,,

[1] Indian advantage in 1872, $1\frac{1}{3}$d.; subtract $1\frac{1}{10}$d., due to fall in freights: add $\frac{3}{10}$d., due to fall in exchange: we get $\frac{7}{10}$d., which is the present advantage (nearly) [*i.e.* in 1893.]

[2] Exact figures not stated; but value of total goods exported to these countries has increased. It is therefore probable that the figure is greater than 113. [See Note 4, p. 151.]

But the only trade she has is in coarse yarns, and there does not seem any immediate prospect of her succeeding in obtaining any other branch of the trade.

Between 1870 and 1886 our exports of yarn and piece goods to India increased considerably.

QUANTITIES EXPORTED TO THE BRITISH EAST INDIES OF COTTON.

Year.	Piece Goods. Million yds.	Yarns. Million lbs.	Year.	Piece Goods. Million yds.	Yarns. Million lbs.
1850	314	21·0	1890	2,190	52·5
1860	825	30·7	1893	1,982	39·9
1870	923	31·0	1896	2,152	52·0
1875	1,231	32·5	1899	2,320	41·4
1880	1,813	47·1	1900	2,019	33·6
1883	1,800	45·3	1901	2,372	37·9
1886	2,238	49·8	1902	2,123	32·5

This increase in value implies a much greater increase in quantity.

Other textiles must be passed by rapidly.

The woollen, our oldest trade, continues to hold an important position. Our home production of raw wool remaining stationary or slightly diminishing, our importations have increased with immense strides to supply the growing demand at home and the increasing quantities needed for export. The price of wool has fallen in the same way as cotton and general commodities; and in spite of this increase in quantity, the value of exports has hardly changed. [See Note 5, p. 152.]

Jute, which has only been of importance since 1860,

and has since then been of great value to Indian trade, has been manufactured in increasing quantities in England, and has counterbalanced the great diminution of flax-spinning which German competition has caused in Ireland; so that the total exportation of jute and linen, yarn and manufactures, have remained stationary in value,[1] increasing in quantity, and diminishing in proportion to our whole trade.

Thus in all textiles our trade has grown, in that we continually increase our exports in bulk, and (all prices falling) obtain more in return. That is, we tend to possess a smaller fraction of the world's manufacturing trade; but, nevertheless, our exports continue to grow in value, as measured by other goods, and in quantity.[2] [See Notes 4 and 5, pp. 151, 152.]

After deducting all coal, metals, steel, machinery, and also all textile manufactures from our total exports, there is a continually growing residuum of miscellaneous goods,[3] which have an important bearing on the aspects of foreign competition.[4]

Taking a final review of our important trades, as shown by the well-known figures of the past few years and the current facts and guesses about future probabilities, we see that, owing to the increasing cost of coal almost certain to arrive sooner or later, our iron and steel trade, depending on the nearness of coal to so great an extent, must continue to sink in comparison with the world's supply. With cotton, on

[1] *I.e.*, value reckoned in £ s. d.

[2] Diagram vi. illustrates this.

[3] Diagram vii., line C.

[4] See next section.

the other hand, the advantages of skill and establishment remain, but no longer as our monopoly; other nations are acquiring both. We have the start, and may keep the lead, but not easily. Moreover, our third advantage, cheap and good coal, may pass, and though continental nations may be worse off than we for coal, India is developing her coalfields, and the United States has large supplies for herself. So far we have only lost part of our trade in coarse yarns; it remains to be seen whether fine yarns will also pass from us.

The possibilities are that the United States will extend her hold over China, the Continent and India continue to supply their increasing wants, and India to press us in the East; while our trade, contracted in some directions, may expand in Africa or elsewhere. We may therefore conclude that there is no immediate fear of our cotton trade rapidly failing us. Old causes continue to help us, and new ones affect others as well as ourselves, and their action must be gradual.

Meanwhile, remembering that it has never in this century been possible to look ten years ahead, that the last things that can be foreseen are a new invention (such as the application of electricity), or a new trade (like the jute manufacture), and that our only safe premise is that any influence displacing capital from textile factories, or reducing the price of cotton goods, will supply a stimulus for finding new employments for capital and new inventions towards economy, we need not give heed too readily to fears that coal and competition are ruining the cotton trade of the country.

3. If we exported nothing, the services of our ships (our "invisible exports") would pay for imports to the amount of £90,000,000,[1] and rank us at once as a second-rate trading power, with only France, Germany, United States (America), Holland, Belgium, and Austria ahead.

There is no need to dwell long on our shipping when we have once realised its importance, because there is no doubt or immediate danger about our supremacy in this direction. The earnings of our merchant service from foreign powers are as great as the value of our cotton exports, and this is a trade on whose continuance we can depend.

The figures of the merchant navies of different countries are so striking that, though well known, they must be given.

Merchant navies (sailing and steam) of—

	1902 1,000 tons.
United Kingdom,	10,055
Colonies and Dependencies of United Kingdom,	1,512
Norway,	1,451
Germany,	2,204
France,	1,218
Italy,	1,019
Japan,	944
United States (Foreign Trade),	883
„ (for Lake, River, and Home Trade),	4,915

The last item illustrates what fifty years ago would have seemed the greatest danger to our supremacy.

[1] The exact figures cannot be given; this is the estimate used by the Board of Trade, Cd., 1761, p. 101.

The United States, with their immense stretch of seaboard and their supply of timber, might have been expected to show their Saxon descent by building the largest navy in the world, and their enormous inland fleet shows their capabilities, but in about 1866 it was decided otherwise.

By the North and South war they were prevented from taking part in the building of steamers, which was then making great progress, and at the end of the war their tariff prevented a cheap supply of steel, which was rapidly becoming of importance; so that, while our merchant fleet became year by year of greater efficiency, and while we, by the rapid construction of vessels that could undertake the new Suez Canal trade, laid the foundation of our modern fleet, the American shipyards rapidly became empty.

As it is, we (including our colonies) own half the ocean service of the world, and have built a new fleet of 740,000 tons for ourselves, and of 180,000 tons for foreigners annually on an average in 1899-1903, while there is hardly a nation in the world that does not employ our ships for the transport of their goods.

2. EXPORTS AND FOREIGN COMPETITION.

In any question affecting the permanence or changes of our foreign trade, it is the distribution and nature of our exports that we must study. For the payment of our exports ultimately we obtain goods, not money; but immediately the dealer obtains a bill of exchange, which answers the same purpose as money, and with which any goods can be obtained from any country. These transactions in the mass, with the mechanism of the exchanges, must balance each other. The important point to notice is that, given a market for exports, we may get exactly what we please in return.

The following table shows the present distribution of our exports.

Exports to the following countries of British and Irish produce—

	1891.	1903.
India and Ceylon,	£31 million.	£34 million.
Australia and New Zealand,	26 "	22 "
North America,	7 "	11 "
Other British Possessions,	22 "	43 "
Total British Possessions,	£86 million.	£110 million.

	1891.	1903.
United States, America,	£27 million.	£22 million.
Europe,	84 "	101 "
Central and South America,	19 "	22 "
China and Japan,	9 "	12 "
Other Foreign Countries	22 "	19 "
Total Foreign Countries,	161 "	176 "
Total Exports,	£247 million.	£286 million.

EUROPE.

	1891.	1903.
Germany, Holland, Belgium,	£35 million.[1]	£40 million.
France,	16 "	16 "
Italy,	6 "	8 "
Spain and Portugal	7 "	7 "
Russia,	5 "	9 "
Sweden and Norway, Denmark and Iceland	7 "	11 "
Other European Countries,	8 "	10 "
	£84 million.	£101 million.

[1] Grouped together because part of the exports to Holland and Belgium are re-exported to Germany.

Thus we see that India is our best customer, followed at no great distance by the United States, Germany, and Australia; and that we export about equal quantities to the whole of our possessions and to Europe.

Next let us notice in what way the proportions of our exports to different districts have been changing.

EXPORTS OF BRITISH AND IRISH PRODUCE.

	1860		1870		1880		1891		1903	
	Value	Percentage	Value	Percentage	Value	Percentage	Value	Percentage	Value	Percentage
	Million		Million		Million		Million		Million	
To Europe, - -	£45	33	£76	38	£82	37	£84	34	£101	35
,, United States, -	21	16	28	14	30	13	27	11	22	8
,, British Possessions,	43	32	51	26	75	34	86	35	110	38
,, Other Countries, -	26	19	44	22	36	16	50	20	53	19
Total - -	£13	100	£199	100	£223	100	£247	100	£286	100

A glance at these tables shows first that the distribution of our exports is co-extensive with the world; and secondly, that, divided on the broadest lines, in spite of all changes, the percentages of exports to the same group have remained almost unchanged.

We will briefly consider the meaning of these figures. Our possessions only take one-third of our exports, and this proportion shows no signs of a rapid increase at present; nor is there any sign of decrease. Natural causes and the freedom of trade have fixed this proportion. In forty years these exports have

DIAGRAM VIII

showing Distribution of Exports of British and Irish Produce.

Quinquennial averages given for Periods 49-52, 53-57, 58-62, 63-67, 68-72 73-77, 78-82, 83-87, 88-92, 93-97, 98-02

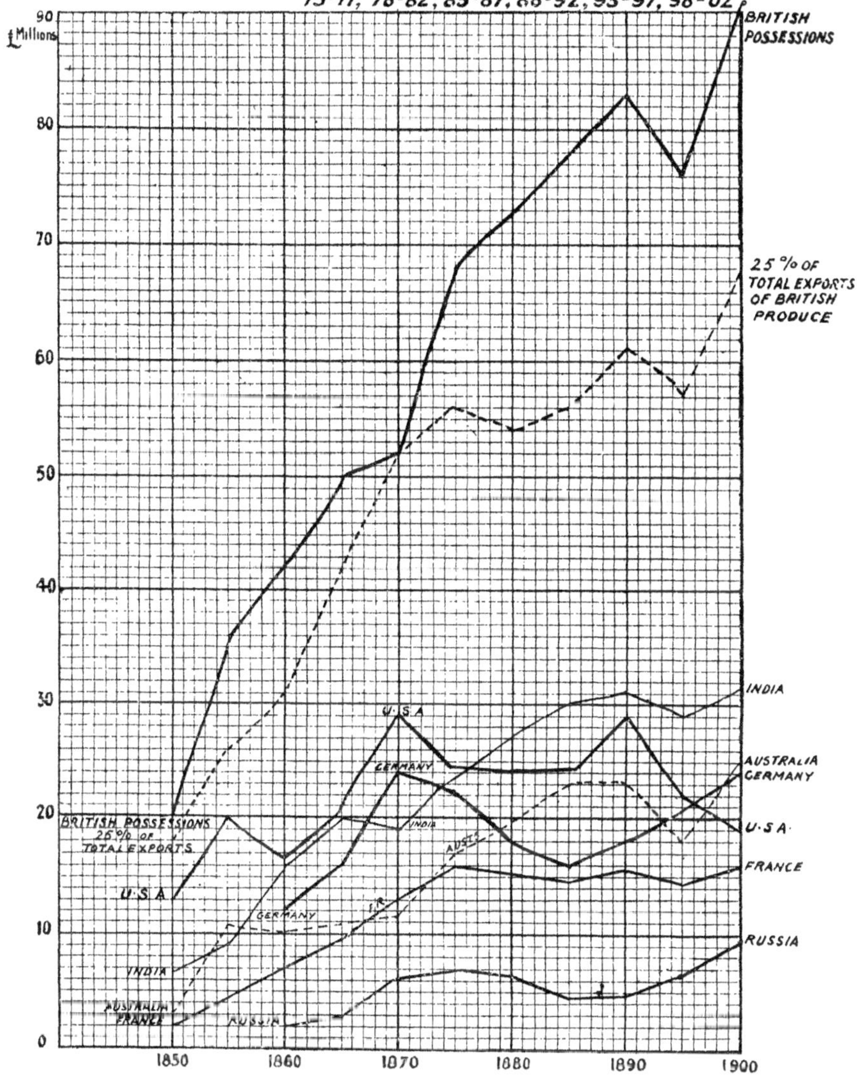

more than doubled in value, and we have the satisfaction of seeing both branches of our trade progressing with equal rapidity. [See Note, p. 149.]

It is important to realise this when any scheme of Imperial federation is under discussion. Any customs union, or commercial arrangement with our colonies, must be an artificial fostering of our colonial relatively to our other trade. Surely the first lesson of these figures is that colonial trade is only of the same importance as European, that during the vicissitudes of thirty years their progress has been the same, and that any tampering with the one in a way which may injure the other can hardly be an advantage to the whole.

That is the first lesson of these figures ; but it is, of course, a very small part of the considerations to be taken into account when dealing with our colonial empire, which we will briefly mention without discussion.

In the future, are our kinsfolk abroad likely to show marked preference for dealing with England, when trade with other countries is equally or more profitable, and will the greater facilities of intercourse in trading with a nation of the same language and customs bring us colonial trade ? Will it be beneficial, if other nations separate themselves into isolated groups by tariffs, to have a vast group of English countries already united, and does this question differ in any way from the general problem of Free Trade ? Is it necessary to take precautions to secure a supply of food in case of war, and if so, would federation be a stronger safeguard than the present vast extent and variety of the sources of our wheat? Would federation strengthen us politically; and finally, do the colonies desire it? [See Note 2, p. 149.]

The changes in the proportions are so slight that slight causes might have produced them; but they give some indication of the broad changes of the conditions of English trade.

The great proportion to British possessions in 1860 reminds us that the gold discoveries were followed by rapid colonial development.

The increment to Europe and to "other countries" in 1870 marks the great railway boom.

The continuous proportionate decrease to the States shows the cumulative effects of their tariff, while the slight percentage fall in the case of Europe is due to the increase of their tariffs and the growth of home manufactures.

This brings us to the general bearing of foreign competition, and the first step towards obtaining clear ideas on the subject is to find under what circumstances foreign manufacture can have any influence on our trade.

The production of goods to be imported to England will be sufficiently considered in the next section. Let us now take in detail production for home consumption (*i.e.*, in the country of the producer) and production for export to neutral markets.[1]

1. The first point to be noticed in the development of manufacture of goods for home consumption, in Germany, for instance, is that each factory is, generally speaking, started with new accumulations of

[1] That is, markets equally open to either country involved.

capital, not with capital withdrawn from old establishments. Thus, many investments were made in manufactures when new capital was flowing into Germany after the Franco-Prussian War. So the old capital used for producing goods to be exported to England is left untouched; an outlet for these goods is still needed, payment must be made directly or indirectly in goods from England, and though some of the goods, hitherto imported from England, are now produced at home, either we are exporting a new class of goods, or there is an increased (German) consumption of the same goods, and the English and German factories are complementary to each other.

The fact that the value of the trade, both exports and imports, between England and Germany has increased 50 per cent. since 1886, while its volume, owing to the fall of prices, has increased more rapidly, shows that some such process has been going on.

The United States supplies a good example. By home manufacture they have diminished our exports to them of steel and tin plates; but they have been sending us continually increasing quantities of wheat and other produce, for which we have been paying by increasing the services of our ships in their trade, and by manufacturing for Eastern countries, who have paid goods to the United States in return instead of to us. It is by such methods as this that capital, displaced by increased manufactures, in other countries finds new occupation; and these broad changes are naturally not realised by those interested in the success of a trade threatened by foreign competition,

The cause of this development of continental trade may be stated in the following way:

Improved agriculture or cheaper supplies of food from other countries has set free a larger proportion of the population for manufacturing and other industries. Since England is or has been the home of all manufactures, some of the surplus labour has necessarily been employed in manufactures that were formerly the monoply of England; becoming richer, they have become better customers, and English work driven out of old channels has continually found new; English capital and enterprise have rarely failed to supply this new demand, and the continual warnings of depression and loss have generally only come from those who, losing their old trade, had not yet found a new outlet; but the whole volume of exports has continually increased. Line C, Diagram vii., shows the increase of exports other than the produce of our great staple trades, while the great length of the list of exported articles, classified in 1893 in the Statistical Abstract under some 120 heads, with a continually growing item for unenumerated miscellaneous goods, points to continuous increase in the variety of our exports.

If, on the other hand, these manufactures are started by capital hitherto employed in other directions, there is necessarily room for us to fill up the gap, and supply, by direct or indirect trade, the goods formerly produced abroad.

If, however, these manufactures are artificially fostered by protection, the country, thus acting, is not richer but poorer rather; they can no longer buy our exports, and we must, with loss, divert our capital to some less profitable employment. There is no doubt that another country can inflict heavy blows on us in this way, that the United States have done so, and that we have no remedy ; the only consolation being that the greater injury to themselves is so apparent, that after a time they may realise it and again open their ports, as there is some prospect of the States now doing. [See Note 3, p. 150.]

The difficulties and loss due to production by other countries for themselves of goods formerly imported from us are thus reduced to the immediate loss due to any change, and to the difficulty of immediately adapting capital and labour to the satisfaction of the new demand, which under normal conditions necessarily exists.

2. The effect of foreign countries manufacturing for exports to neutral markets is *mutatis mutandis* the same. If the world is richer, if new capital is being used for production, there can be no diminution, only changes in distribution of trade. But in this case two difficulties, one temporary, the other permanent, become prominent, and they cannot be explained away.

In spite of increased wealth and increased demand, over-production is very easy. If a new factory is started by the side of old ones, though the world may be rich enough to buy the produce of both, yet its wants in that direction may not be developed, the channels of distribution may not be free, and the price at which it is willing to take the new supply may be too small to be remunerative ; or a mistake may have been made altogether as to the class of goods which the new wealth demanded, and merely an excess of articles with which the world was well provided may have been produced. This dead-lock is in each individual case speedily removed, but, of course, each mistake will exact some pecuniary penalty.

Again, though the increasing wealth, evidenced by increasing manufactures, will create a new or an altered demand, which England has the chance of satisfying, this new demand is in these days of free commerce and competition made impartially to the whole world, the country where trade has been displaced having only the advantage of unemployed labour and capital set free from its old trade. That is to say, that each change is a step towards the division of labour, a new prize offered to the most competent to supply the wants of mankind. For this prize it is quite possible that England may not be a successful competitor. Let us examine the qualifications for success. There is needed an accurate knowledge of the goods required, a rapid adaptation of fixed and floating capital and labour to their production, and suitable climatic conditions; then, if these things are equal, the country, where interest and profits are lowest, and labour (measured by its efficiency) cheapest, wins.

What are England's chances in this competition? Taking the factors in the same order, investigation of foreign requirements is not carried to the same extent as other nations find possible;[1] capital is very

[1] Why should not our consular reports be equal to those of the States, or our travellers as active as the Germans?

easily moved, new methods are soon understood and perfected, and the English artisan, with his skill and common sense, very soon understands new machinery, while England's compactness allows rapid migration to the best seat of industry. England's climate is eminently suited for continuous hard work, and her supply of coal has hitherto given her the advantage over every other nation. Capital is so plentiful that interest has rapidly fallen; while profits have been cut down by the stress of competition, since no handicap in this direction could be afforded.

There remains the item of wages, which are higher in England than in any European or Asiatic country. But it is not the value of each man's wages, but the amount of work done for a given quantity of wages, that is in question.

Many business men hold the opinion expressed by an American manufacturer thus—"If a difference in rates of wages establishes itself in a manufacture, between two places allowed to trade freely, the business is more likely to go to the one paying higher wages, than to leave it for the one paying lower," and the reason for this is a double one. First, from the purely economical point of view, if a man succeeds in obtaining high wages it is because his increased work and skill is cheaper at that price than inferior work and skill at a lower price. Secondly, the effect of high wages is to make the recipients of them more civilised, more manly and trustworthy, stronger and better, mentally, morally, and physically. The mere statement of this fact goes far to remove the idea that the competition of badly paid labour will necessarily be injurious.

To support this view many figures could be given, but the following (referring to 1893) will be sufficient.

Wages in Mexico are 10 to 15 cents a day, in New England about a dollar a day. New England competes successfully with Mexico.

Wages in factories are low in Switzerland, fairly high in England, higher in America; but the number of looms run by one man in the three countries are two, three or four, and six or eight respectively.

America is afraid of the competition of "English paupers" just in the same way as we are of continental labour; yet we fear American competition.

Wages in Bombay are far lower than wages in Manchester; but Bombay, with all its efforts, has only obtained part of one particular class of cotton spinning.

Wages vary immensely in agricultural districts all over the world; but no country is making exceptionally large profits on the corn it exports.

These facts are sufficient to prove that badly-paid labour is not necessarily the most profitable; but the following considerations must also be taken into account:

First, if wages increase faster than the corresponding increase in efficiency in one country, and at the same pace in another, the former is handicapped.

Secondly, if the supply of food and other necessaries is cheaper in Brittany, for instance, than in England, this has its full effect in keeping wages lower in the former. Any comparison of wages without allowing for this fact is perfectly useless; wages must be measured by the amount of the necessaries and luxuries of life which they will purchase ; that is, those necessaries and luxuries which are customary in the country of the workman, whether it be the United States, England, Germany, India, or China. If this consideration is neglected, the same mistakes will be made that are so frequent in casual comparisons of wages at different periods in England.

Thirdly, if the standard of living is higher in England than in France, it probably means that better living has its natural effect in better work, but it may mean that the French spend less on useless luxuries than the English.

English labour is well organised, and cannot easily be exploited by the capitalist: continental labourers are imperfectly combined, and more at the mercy of their employers. Thus the Continent has at present the doubtful advantage of cheap labour from this source also. But there are continual efforts being made in Belgium, Germany, and France on the part of workmen to raise their status and their wages towards the English standard; and these efforts will be more successful as these countries become more wealthy. In the long run real wages in different countries will tend to equality (*i.e.*, equal wages for equal quantities of work), just as they have in different towns in the same country.

There appear, then, to be no valid grounds for fear of a general reduction of English wages towards the continental standard. But, when the stress of competition in particular trades makes itself felt, when profits are cut down, prices diminished, and every economy practised, the workmen in both competing countries bear their part of the strain. If the other country is destined to win, wages and profits will diminish to the lowest possible point before the battle is lost. When the struggle is decided, as we have already shown, there will be new openings for the workmen, and average wages in the whole country will be as before; we have only the familiar sequence of changes which always follow a change of industrial conditions, whether the influences at work are confined to one country or involve several.

Before we can admit that English foreign trade can be diminished, we must admit that foreign nations have sufficient capital and labour to spare (which in reality would take a generation or more to accumulate) to undertake our industries, that England can lose her compactness and her highly finished organisation and multifarious division of labour, that English enterprise and courage is failing, that the energy, common sense and inherited skill of the English labourer is deserting him, that we have no resources but coal, can succeed in no manufacture but cotton, and shall lose command of the seas, and, more marvellous still, that some other nation will obtain and keep these advantages. The history of the nineteenth century teaches no such lesson.

But if, in the distant future, increased skill, or new discoveries, or natural advantages give to some other country the position so long enjoyed by us, if, as the great process of world-wide division of labour takes its inevitable course, it is found that in England few industries can find a place that are not undertaken better elsewhere, it will mean that

DIAGRAM IX.

showing Character of Imports, 1854-1904.

A. Value of Imports, less re-exports.
B. " " " of Food & Wine, less re-exports.
C. " " " Raw Textile Materials, less re-exports.

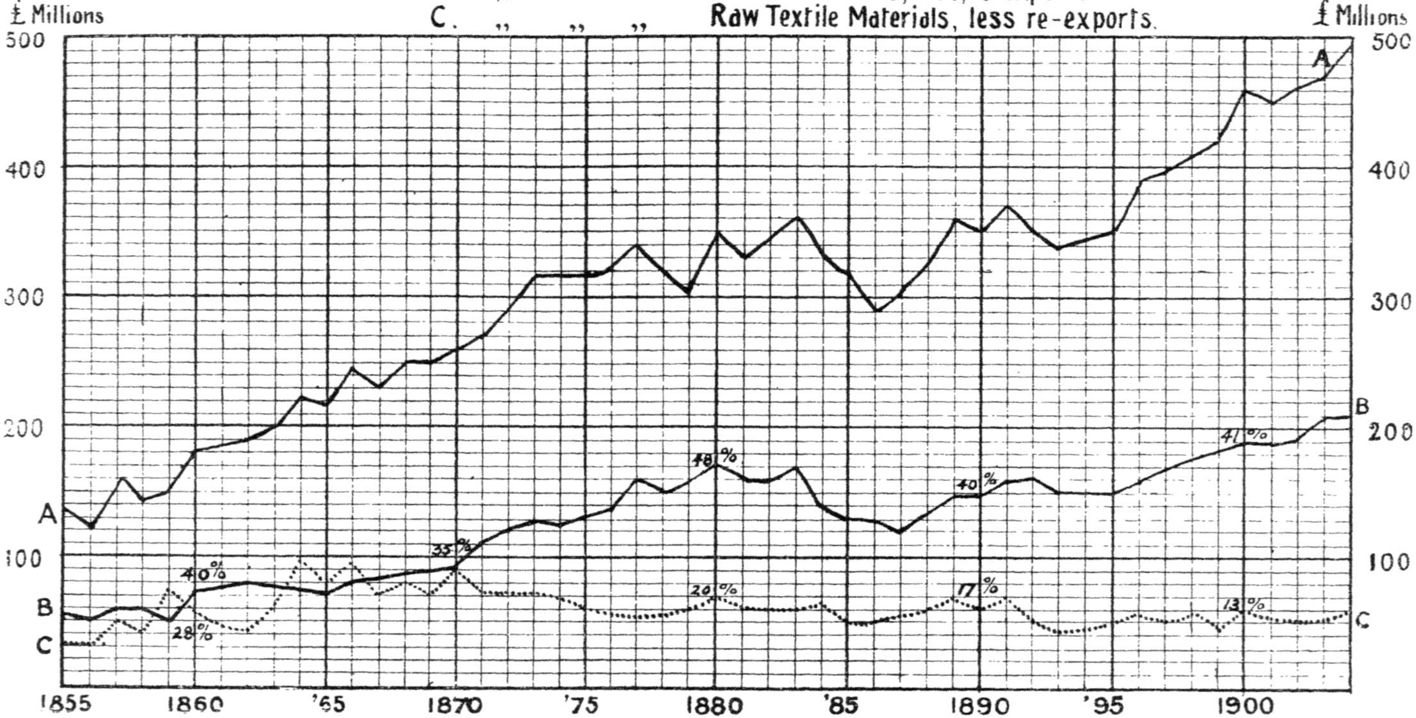

Englishmen will gradually forsake the home country, that English enterprise will be successful in some other quarter of the globe, and that England will still be the home and mother of successful and multitudinous offspring.

3. IMPORTS AND AGRICULTURE.

Our foreign trade is to a great extent an elaborate machinery for supplying us with food. Of the £470 millions'-worth of goods which come to our share, at least £200 millions'-worth is food; while £115 millions'-worth is of raw materials, which can be definitely reckoned, and of the remaining £155 millions, if it was possible to distinguish materials for manufacture from materials for sale, part would be found to be materials for our factories, rather than goods for consumption.

Let us consider how this enormous annual bill for food is paid, regarding the whole nation as a single family. Tabulating imports and exports thus:—

IMPORTS FOR CONSUMPTION OR MANUFACTURE, ROUGHLY GROUPED.

	Annual Average. 1898-1902.
Food	£190 million.
Wine and Tobacco, ...	10 ,,
Raw Textiles, ...	55 ,,
Other Raw Materials and Articles, mainly unmanufactured, ...	75 ,,
Articles mainly Manufactured, ...	110 ,,
	£440 ,,
Interest on Capital (approximate estimate)	85 ,,
	£355 million,

to be paid by exports, and earnings of shipping.

EXPORTS OF HOME PRODUCE.

	Annual Average. 1898-1902.
Textile Products, ...	£100 million.
Iron and Steel and their Products, ...	50 ,,
Coal, ...	30 ,,
Other Merchandise	90 ,,
	£270 ,,
Earnings of Shipping (approximate estimate), ...	85 ,,
	£355 million.

In the manufacture of textiles, so great is the increase of value, that after the home market has been supplied, the exports of yarn and cloth are worth £45,000,000 more than the raw materials. The cotton workers thus pay for the raw cotton we use at home, and have this surplus towards our food supply.

Workers in mines, iron foundries, steel, machinery, etc., add to the value of the ores extracted and the ores and metals imported to such an extent that we are supplied, and a surplus of £50,000,000 is ready to pay for imports.

These sums added to the earnings of our ships go far to make up the £190,000,000 sufficient to cover our bill for provisions.

This done, we may reckon that half the miscellaneous goods imported are in return for miscellaneous exports, while the other half are the interest due on our foreign investments.

We do not mean to imply that the destination of our textiles is the country which supplies our corn, with similar conditions for the other case; but only to supply data for comparing the relative importance

DIAGRAM X
shewing Sources of Imports.
Quinquennial averages given for periods
1854-57, 58-62, 63-67, 68-72, 73-77, 78-82, 83-87, 88-92 93-97, 98-02.

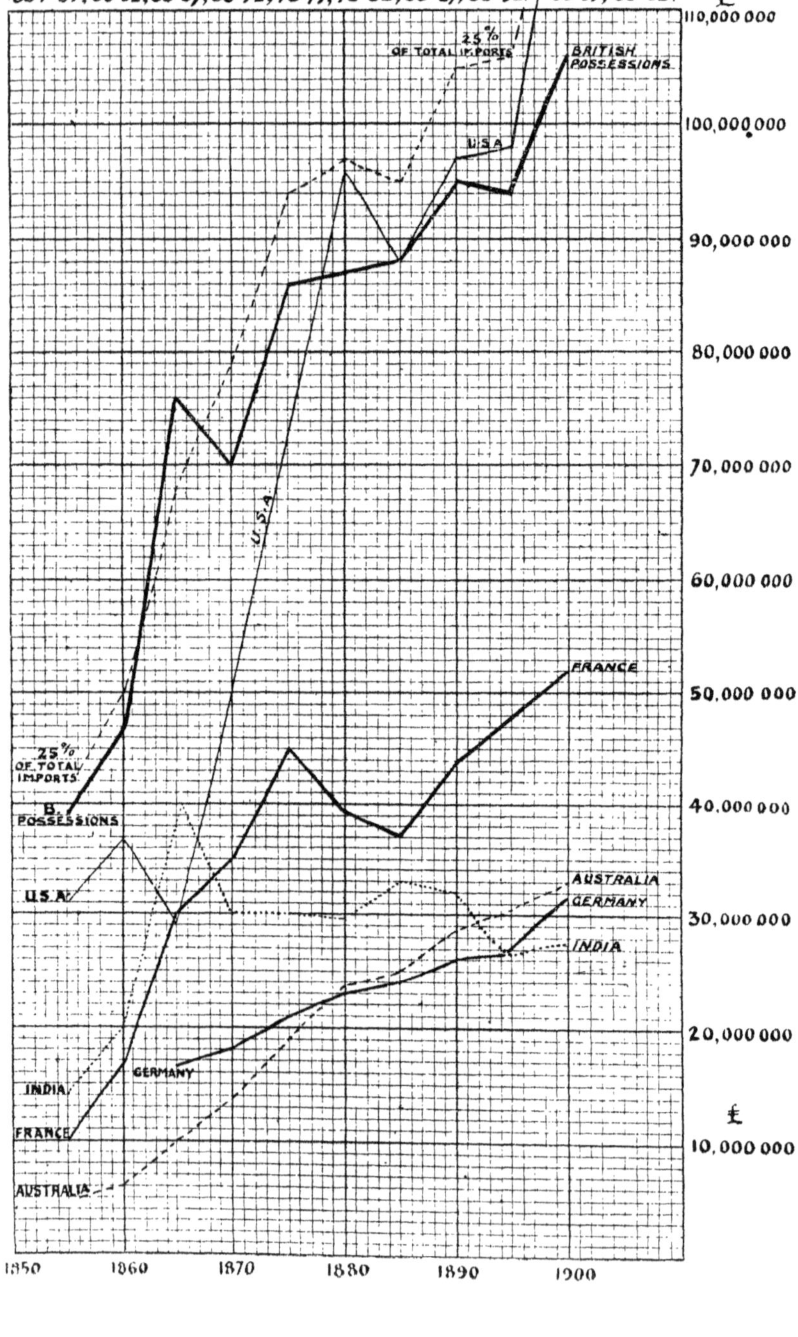

of different trades. As a matter of fact, our exports do not always go to the countries from which we obtain imports. The United States are paid for their corn partly by manufactures, partly by goods from China and other countries, who thus pay their debts to us. Again, food imports are often the payment of interest on capital invested; and in many cases it is not easy to trace the equilibrium of trade. The broad result is a balancing of all the individual transactions, accomplished by bills of exchange on individual dealers, and involving an infinitude of operations.

The quantity of imports which we obtain for home consumption is the measure of the benefit of our trade. Imports may be divided into two classes (between which, however, there is no distinct line of demarcation), those which we could obtain by home growth or manufacture, and those which we could not.

Selecting the largest items from a list of imports for consumption or manufacture (so as to tabulate about three-quarters of the whole), we find :—

	Annual Average. 1898-1902.
Wool, ...	£15 million.
Other Raw Textiles, ...	55 ,,
Grain and Meal, ...	50 ,,
Fish, Meat, Animals, ...	50 ,,
Tea, Coffee, Sugar, Wine, Spirits, and Tropical Produce, ...	60 ,,
Dairy Produce, ...	35 ,,
Ores and Unwrought Metals, ...	20 ,,
Timber, ...	25 ,,
Textile Manufactures, ...	30 ,,
	£340 million.

Now select those goods which we could not obtain at home, *viz.*:—

Cotton, Silk, Jute, etc., ...	...	...	...	£54 million.
Tropical Produce, etc., ...	...	...	...	62 "
Ores and Unwrought Metals, ...		...	...	20 "

or less, for our mines could be more fully worked ; or about three-eighths of the goods enumerated.

With regard to these, no one can have any doubt as to the benefits of trade.

We can grow timber and corn, supply butter, eggs, cheese, and meat, and manufacture silk ; but the proof of the benefit of importing them is three-fold. In the first place, no one will buy foreign goods if he can obtain those more to his taste or at a lower price of home growth ; hence the fact that they are bought proves the existence of advantage. Secondly, no foreigner will send us goods unless he can obtain from England or England's debtors produce which he prefers to that of his own growth ; in which case it follows that our labourers are engaged in some occupation more advantageous both to us and our customers than those in question. Thirdly, there are all the reasons summed up in the phrase "diminishing return," which may be thus explained. It may very well be possible that by improved methods and conditions, and enterprise well directed, some part of the demand for dairy produce, say, could be secured for English farmers ; but the magnitude of the figures shows that though more pasture land might reduce the importation of meat, or more arable ground the importation of corn, it would be impossible to produce grain, meat, wool, dairy produce, and wood from the soil sufficient for home needs. Moreover, after the first possible trifling alterations had been made, after more attention had been given, for instance, to fruit or to cheese, and the larger problem of growing corn was attacked, it is obvious that the soil that does not now pay when sown must be used; that each increase in this direction would mean the utilisation of more and more inferior soil, or the placing on better soil a burden greater than it could bear without injury, or without more careful and laborious attention; that, in fact, as more grain was demanded, increasing labour for each new increment would be necessary, and the price would rise with each increase of supply. This is what is meant by the law of diminishing return.

We thus see that, from the point of view of economy in purchasing food, as a nation we have reason to be glad that corn-growing country is becoming pasture land, or going out of cultivation; it means that the price of grain is falling, and that we can obtain supplies more cheaply from other countries. It also means that there is an increase of employment in other occupations, for no one will send us corn without payment, which can only be made by exportation of goods. Money does not "go out of the country," nor go "to the foreigner instead of to the English," it merely goes to the artisan or the factory hand instead of to the agricultural labourer. The result is pure gain pecuniarily to the country as a whole; work is applied in directions which give the greatest return. It remains to consider the effect on farmers, and the social effect on the country of this migration of labour, and then to discuss the future possibilities of change in this direction.

The complete discussion of the agricultural question would need a book to itself; all that is possible here is to sum up the historical aspect of it.

The days of the Corn Laws were a golden time for landlords, as was the war for farmers. All the corn that could be grown obtained a ready sale, and in a time of scarcity fortunes could be made at the expense of the suffering nation. The usual penalties for trade artificially aided were exacted from the next generation of landlords. Rents had been fixed on the basis of the old system, and were not modified sufficiently till incalculable mischief had been done; landlords would not, and till this day do not fully, recognise that English soil cannot bear the burden of heavy rents in competition with cheap land abroad. Farmers had drifted into the extravagant habits usually begotten by prosperity, and were neglecting the knowledge of their trade. Notwithstanding the great progress of the science of agriculture at the end of the eighteenth century, the land was injudiciously used, and exhausted to obtain great crops for the current high prices.

In spite of these handicaps, agriculture continued a prosperous undertaking, compared with other investments, for many years after the repeal; and the cries of distress were due to the fall of prices, not to a low level, but from the artificial height to which tariffs had raised them.

From about 1870 onwards, however, English

agriculture was seriously attacked. The competition of new countries, where land could be had almost for the asking, where in some cases, such as Russia and India, labour was cheap; in others where the soil yielded a crop after but little work; in others where pioneers in the West did not mind whether they made a profit or not, provided they established a claim to the land, which they could sell when advancing population raised its value—this competition found England unprepared. Some of her soil is the finest for wheat-growing in the world, in the sense that sufficient labour will produce the most luxuriant harvest from a given area; but then there was also inferior land under cultivation. Then, in all cases, landlords expected rent greater than could be afforded under the new conditions, and English labour, even agricultural, is not cheap, compared with continental or Eastern countries. Thus a steady fall of prices has set in, agriculture in the most favourable districts does not pay as it used, in the worse districts does not pay at all, and there are no extra profits to be made in seasons of scarcity at home, for all the world is ready to fill up our deficits.

During this time there has naturally been a relative diminution of agricultural labourers, since a larger proportion of our workmen is required to pay for imported food, and in some districts an actual diminution, owing partly to the changing of arable into pasture land (which is still profitable), and partly to the higher wages or superior attractions of town. But, as a matter of fact, agricultural wages have not fallen; they have during the century steadily risen as a whole; they have only increased less rapidly than wages of artisans. The loss has fallen almost exclusively on landlords and farmers. It is always a melancholy spectacle to see the suffering or ruin of a class which necessarily accompanies any change and improvement in trade; it is the heavy price which must invariably be paid for progress; the hand-worker loses when machinery is introduced, the small manufacturer is ruined when the large factory is established, old occupations must give way to new and profitable trades, and in the next generation the distress passes, and the old customs are forgotten.

Nevertheless, it is not certain yet that English agriculture cannot improve; rents may be further reduced, land may be used for its most profitable products, fruit, or dairy produce, or meat (of constantly increasing importance as the urban population grows in size and wealth), inequalities of transport and freight may be removed, and large country districts be in the most flourishing condition. There is a limit to the virgin land which can be taken up. When and before that is reached, land now cultivated must be made by extra labour to produce greater harvests, more work will be needed for the growth of wheat, prices must rise. With increasing population the States will have less to export to us. The law of "diminishing return" must some day apply to the whole world; and it seems probable that the day must come when we shall see the series of agricultural changes of this generation reversed in England; land, let out of cultivation, again utilised, prices rising, and agriculture prosperous.

One important effect of this, the most characteristic and important phenomenon due to our foreign trade, remains to be mentioned. In England especially, in all countries which have taken to manufacturing to a less extent, in the States, in Germany and in France, the country population tends to be a diminishing proportion of the whole, while the towns increase. In the broadest sense this means that, owing to the introduction of machinery in farming, and the application of science, less labour is needed to produce each man's food, and the world can spare more and more energy for other productions. Meanwhile, we are exchanging the health and the subtle influences of country life for the bustle, strain, unsanitary conditions and crowding of towns; and unless the Utopian scheme (less favoured by modern economists than by the philosophers of the sixteenth century) of alternate changes from town to country labour of each family is adopted, unless "many of them take such pleasure in agriculture that they desire leave to continue in it many years,"[1] grave effects are to be feared on the physique and health of the English race.

4. CONCLUSION.

The growth of our foreign trade has had so many intricate and far-reaching effects in every phase of our political, social, and individual life, and in every

[1] More's "Utopia." (The modern interpretation would be that the children of citizens should migrate to the country, the children of country-folk to the town.)

department of business, that it is not easy to sum them up.

The first effect on individual incomes is sufficiently obvious; money will often go further when laid out in foreign goods than in native. It is not easy to make the comparison, because the corresponding home goods disappear from the market; but each article of foreign growth or manufacture, *e.g.*, corn, meat, alarum clocks, when first offered for sale was at a lower price than the English produce, and we have gained in all these goods the whole difference between the English and foreign prices. We have no means of estimating this gain, but the goods thus cheapened have been sufficiently numerous to account for nearly one-quarter[1] of our private expenditure. Of course, we have the further advantage of greatly increased variety. We may at the same price buy cheese from Canada, Holland, or Cheddar; we can have the fruit and wine of every country, and metals from any mine in the world. So great is the variety of goods imported, and from so many sources do they come, that very few people could say definitely, in looking round an ordinary room, which things in it had no foreign workmanship in them.

The benefit of this increase of purchasing power has not been equally distributed; it has come mainly to the working classes and to people with small incomes. Our imports consisting so largely of food, it is those who have to consider every penny expended in housekeeping who are enriched by the reductions in price of bread, meat, and rice. Since

[1] The exact fraction is not known, even approximately.

the era of foreign trade there are hardly any in regular employment so poor that they cannot obtain as much bread as they want of a finer quality than middle-class people at the begining of the century; meat is no longer a rare luxury among any large class of workmen as it was fifty years ago; it is only necessary to allude to the reductions in price of tea, sugar, jam, foreign cheese, clothing materials, and other commodities which bulk largely in a working-class budget. At the same time a variety of food is possible, which must conduce greatly to the health and pleasure of city life.

The wealthy have, of course, gained the same advantages as the poor, but since bread, meat, fruit, and wine are at their command at whatever price they may be, the boon has been comparatively slight to them.

As we saw at the commencement, foreign trade was first the result of inventions and then the cause of further inventions. We must credit to foreign trade a large part of the cheapness and variety of goods of home manufacture. Consider, for instance, the effect of modern inventions in the cotton manufacture. An improvement is made in spinning: almost instantaneously America and India learn the new method, and by competition of foreign manufactures English customers and the whole world at once get the full benefit of the new economy: it is rarely that they now have to wait till a patent expires. Foreign competition first stimulates the inventive faculties of the manufacturer, and then gives us at once the full advantage of inventions, the inventor still obtaining some reward by being first in the field. In short, the benefits of the Industrial Revolution to home trade could not have been secured without the indirect influence of foreign trade.

The effects of the growth of foreign trade on the relations between nation and nation have been as great politically as they have been commercially. The final influence which trade will have on war is not yet determined. Nations are now inter-dependent; the sudden isolation of any one by war or by tariffs would revolutionise the trade of many others. A war that hindered our merchant service would quickly produce such distress as would necessitate a rapid conclusion of peace, and though other countries would suffer in the same manner, their foreign trade is not so developed that its cessation would have equally disastrous effects. This view exaggerates the insecurity of our position; for, though our dependence on importation for our supply of food would make our suffering markedly acute, yet the advantage of our trade is as great to our customers as to ourselves, and its hindrance would after a short time be ruinous to them. The advocates of peace have gained a very strong argument from this addition to the horrors and dangers of war.

England's start in the development of trade has given her a unique position in the commercial world: the dignity of her position has risen during the century: fifty years ago she was the storekeeper for Europe of the goods of the East and the Tropics; she has ceased to hold that office, owing to the development of transport and means of communication, but her capital and credit have made her the banker of the world.

So far we have glanced at the pleasant aspects of foreign trade, so familiar as to need only a brief recapitulation, and we have seen such increase of wealth and efficiency of labour as will outweigh any evils we may find on the reverse of the picture; nevertheless, there are evils to be faced, though good is interspersed even amongst them.

The effects of the world-extension of trade on general business have been an acceleration of pace, an accompanying increase of risk (with counterbalancing effects such as the improvement of communication, which tend to security), a great development of competition with its evils as well as its benefits, and an endless complication of interests, methods, and chances.

The regular occurrence of commercial depressions is a phenomenon known before the era of foreign trade, but these depressions are now more far-reaching, of longer duration, and of more involved and doubtful origin than formerly. The result is a sinking of profits, with long-delayed reaction, and great difficulty in foreseeing and calculating effects. A new uncertainty is introduced into trade, the vast complication is almost beyond the ken of the keenest men of business. And, while the whole system of trade is continually changing, the more important of all the adjustments of business is left to chance, which theoretically arranges all these matters on the best of all possible systems, but actually leaves much to be desired. While competition for leave to manufacture and sell is so great, that with the suffering of the manufacturer the public is served with the cheapest and best goods, the competition for leave to work and obtain wages is so keen that that public can hardly find vent for its energies and obtain the means to buy. The increase of each man's power of production appears to have been greater than the increase of production itself. The great machine has been improved so fast that fewer men are needed to work it; and since only those who receive wages for work or interest from profits can purchase its products, we have particular machines tending to produce more than customers are ready to buy. Our system of trade has developed so fast that we are no longer able to manage it. Men become better and better qualified for every branch of work (except, indeed, for the quiet, peaceful, and old-fashioned industries), but for each vacant post, whether for intellectual, clerical, or mechanical work, the number of competitors is out of all proportion to that required.

Even if we wished to pause we could not. There is no possibility of a world-wide arrangement of production or of division of labour other than natural causes or chance dictate. We cannot make any really great deviation from the established rule of free industry and competition without damaging our foreign trade. We must continue in the race, and we may comfort ourselves with this reflection—in all our investigations we have found no essential point in which foreign trade differs from home trade except in its greater complication. Home trade has long been subject to the strain of competition, and we have been steadily growing richer, keeping the advantages we have gained and finding employment and wages for the great mass of the people: the competition from foreign trade has had less time for adjustment, its great benefits already far exceed the loss and worry due to change and unsettling; and we may hope that we shall become accustomed to the pace and masters of the method of modern business, as earlier in the century we became used to factories and masters of the organisation of machinery.

We are still at the commencement of the growth of international trade. Only a fraction, perhaps one-fifth, of British capital and labour is invested in the carrying on of foreign trade; with improvements of communication and knowledge, and decrease of prejudice, there is no reason why division of labour among nations should not be brought to as great perfection as division among different districts of England, why each country should produce for itself more than a fraction of the moveable goods it requires.

The history of this century may be repeated; nations learn to be at peace with one another, if the burden of vast armies and the sense of the silent majority induce disarmament; the advantages of Free Trade may be rediscovered; as steam and mechanical inventions in this century, so electricity and physics in the next may further increase man's power over nature; and perhaps we shall see the beginning of an expansion of foreign trade, which will surpass even the unprecedented growth of this century.

APPENDIX TO REVISED EDITION, 1905.

Note 1.—FREE TRADE.

SEE pp. 41-46.—It seemed best to leave the treatment of the principles of Free Trade exactly as published in the First Edition. Recent controversy has brought into prominence considerations which call for additional comment.

As regards Section 5, p. 42.—It is supposed by many that an increase of imports diminishes home employment. Now, imports must either come (α) in payment of debt, or (β) as loans to be repaid in the future, or (γ) be paid for almost at once by exports or other services ; in other words, they must correspond to past, present, or future exports or other services. A study of our trade statistics shows that more gold comes into the United Kingdom than leaves it, and the quantity is insignificant compared with the whole value of our trade, so that the great part of the balance is to be made by exports of goods and other services. These other services are mainly the work done by our merchant navy, and by the financiers and agents in London, who are intermediaries in many wholly-foreign trade transactions.

As regards (α) and (β), the evidence goes to show that we have almost continuously increased our net investments abroad (except perhaps in the time of the South African war), and that there has been a regularly increasing flow of interest to us. As regards (γ), the services of our ships appear to have increased steadily. Apart from these, we are left with a steady volume of imports which must in the main be paid for by a steady volume of exports, and any change in one must produce a change in the other. Imports are not then *necessarily* connected with any diminution in the amount of home employment. On the other hand, the kind of employment needed, and the date at which services are to be rendered, is affected by every change in any of the factors that go to make the balance ; but this continual change does not differ from the changes induced by variations of credit and of demand in internal trade. Whether the enlargement of the field of transactions tends to steady employment, or the reverse, is a matter of dispute.

As regards Section 6, p. 42.—Many economists hold that the German industrial policy has benefited German trade, home and foreign. This, from the nature of the case, can neither be proved nor disproved. It may happen that unlimited competition may give immediate benefit to the individual, at the future expense of the nation, as trade may be directed on lines which lead to rapid advantage, but diminish the chance of more permanent returns ; it is conceivable that a wise government could hinder this tendency, but the practical difficulties of deciding what transactions come under this head, and of checking them without unforeseen and injurious complications, seem to the present writer insuperable.

The main justification for a so-called "National Policy" is to be found in the last paragraph of page 15, and the paragraph beginning "It is often thought . . ." on page 43. These are left as in the First Edition, except that the words "or the country" are added, p. 16, l. 5.

Note 2.—Colonial Preference.

See pp. 121, 124.—The paragraphs relating to Imperial federation are left exactly as in the First Edition. The question has developed a good deal since then. In 1898 Canada, and in 1903 Cape Colony, gave a preference to the home country (that is, allowed dutiable goods to enter at rates below the ordinary tariff). The proposal has been made that the various members of the British Empire shall make general and special agreements to give preference to each other's goods. This involves the necessity that those members (including the United Kingdom) whose trade is now on a Free Trade basis shall re-arrange their tariff so as to make reductions from it possible ; *e.g.*, that we should put a tax on foreign wheat in order to make a reduction in favour of Colonial wheat. This would, of course, involve protection to those home products which were of the same kind as imported Colonial products. At the same time, a tariff of this nature would make it easy to retaliate on foreign countries who treated our goods adversely. Colonial preference has thus become involved with protection of home industries, and with a bellicose attitude in trade matters towards foreign countries. The alternative scheme of giving bounties on imported Colonial goods, which would give a preference to the Colonies without protection at home, has not received support. Modern arguments for protection in the United Kingdom do not differ in the main from those outlined on pages 43, 44, and developed in Note 1, above.

Note 3.—Changes in Foreign Tariffs.

See pp. 62, 67, 68, 69, 70, 71, 127.—In U.S.A. the "McKinley" Tariff of 1890 was replaced by the "Wilson" Tariff in 1894, by which duties were reduced; but in 1897 another change was made, and the "Dingley" Tariff brought duties up to a very high level. The exports of British and Irish produce to U.S.A. were valued at—

	1890	1891	1892	1893	1894	1895	1896
Million	£32	28	26	24	19	28	20
	1897	1898	1899	1900	1901	1902	1903
Million	£21	15	18	20	18	24	22

In Prussia duties were reduced in 1862, in the Zollverein in 1865. The German Empire was constituted in 1871. In 1879 the German Tariff was raised to a strongly protective level, and it was increased further in 1885. There was some reduction in 1891, but the tariff remained at a high level, which was raised especially on agricultural products by a general revision in 1902, coming into force in 1905 or 1906.

In France the "Cobden" Treaty of 1860 governed the tariff till 1882, when some duties were increased and others reduced. A considerable increase followed in 1892.

The Board of Trade estimates (Cd. 2337, p. 292) the *ad valorem* equivalent of the Import Duties levelled on the principal manufactures exported from the United Kingdom in 1903-4 as follows:—

Russia, 131; United States, 73; France, 34; Germany, 25; Canada, 17; Belgium, 13; New Zealand, 9; Japan, 9; Switzerland, 7; Australia, 6; South Africa, 6; Holland, 3; British India, 3.

Note 4.—COTTON.

See pp. 66, 93, 112-115.—Since 1893 the consumption of cotton in the United Kingdom has increased, the average for 1898-1902 being 15 million cwts., while that for 1889-93 was 14·1 million cwts. The world's consumption of cotton has tended to outstrip the supply, and there was a serious shortage in 1903-04 when the supply from U.S.A. fell off. Three-quarters to four-fifths of the whole supply still comes from U.S.A., but efforts are now being made to extend the cultivation of cotton in the British Empire. The value of exported cotton manufactures (1893-1904) showed no important changes that were not accounted for by changes in the price of raw cotton. The quantity of piece goods has increased, but not so rapidly as prior to 1890; that of yarns has fallen off.

EXPORTS OF COTTON.

Average of years.	Piece goods. Million yards.	Yarns. Million lbs.
1883-1887	4620	255
1888-1892	4970	250
1893-1897	5000	240
1898-1902	5160	190

It is supposed that the piece-goods are of increasing intrinsic value, so that the increase is rather greater than appears. Europe is taking less than in former periods, as Germany and other countries develop their home manufactures and protect them by tariffs, but U.S.A. is taking more. [See Cd. 1761, pp. 444, 115.] No foreign country has as yet made very much impression on neutral markets; but Germany, Belgium, Switzerland, and U.S.A. together exported in 1900 cotton goods of not far less than half the value of the cotton exports from the United Kingdom. India exported (average of 1896-1900)

£4,600,000 worth of twist and yarn, and £1,800,000 worth of manufactures (reckoning £1=15 rupees).

Note 5.—Wool.

See p. 116.—The consumption of wool in the United Kingdom has increased very rapidly in recent years; but the value and quantity of exports have fallen off, while production for the home market has increased.

EXPORTS OF WOOL.

00,000 omitted.

Average.	Manufactures.		Yarn.		Consumption of Wool in United Kingdom.
1883-1892.	£195	235 yds.	£52	542 lbs.	4181 lbs.
1893-1902.	158	168 ,,	63	727 ,,	5145 ,,

It seems almost certain that the falling off in number of yards is partly explained by the greater intrinsic worth of each, the average weight and fineness increasing. The quantity exported to U.S.A. increased very much in 1895, during the Wilson Tariff, but has been at a low level since the Dingley Tariff of 1897. The quantity exported to Germany, Holland, and Belgium together remained stationary from 1890 to 1900, but fell in 1901-03; that to France has fallen rapidly. Meanwhile the importation of woollen cloths has increased, till the total value of woollen yarns and manufactures imported into the United Kingdom is nearly half that of exports of similar goods. The woollen and worsted trade is so differentiated in the various countries and towns manufacturing them, that this double trade is less remarkable than appears at first sight. The exports of competing countries to neutral markets is of considerable extent; but the value of the German export trade was the same in 1890 and 1900, while that of France fell off.

Note 6.—Iron and Steel.

See pp. 90, 108-111.—The production of pig-iron in the twenty years, 1882-1901, has been—

	Average for Quinquennial Periods.			
	1882-86	1887-91	1892-96	1897-1901
	Tons.	Tons.	Tons.	Tons.
United Kingdom	7,900,000	7,800,000	7,500,000	8,700,000
United States ...	4,600,000	7,600,000	8,200,000	12,800,000
Germany	3,500,000	4,400,000	5,400,000	7,700,000
France	1,800,000	1,800,000	2,100,000	2,500,000

The total consumption of pig-iron, domestic and foreign, has been in the same periods—

	1882-86	1887-91	1892-96	1897-1901
	Tons.	Tons.	Tons.	Tons.
United Kingdom.	6,600,000	6,800,000	6,700,000	7,700,000
United States ...	4,900,000	7,700,000	8,200,000	12,800,000
Germany	3,600,000	4,600,000	5,500,000	8,300,000
France	2,000,000	1,800,000	2,000,000	2,700,000

The United Kingdom is thus falling to the third place in this respect. The manufacture of machinery and many other products depending on iron and steel has, however, increased rapidly at home, and an increasing export trade has been done in machinery.

EXPORTS OF CERTAIN IRON AND STEEL PRODUCTS FROM THE UNITED KINGDOM.

	Quinquennial Averages.				
	1885-89	1890-94	1895-99	1900-04	
Cutlery, hardware, implements, and tools............	£3·9	3·5	3·4	3·9	millions
Machinery	14	14	15	19	,,
Miscellaneous iron and steel products	21	20	18	23·6	,,
Ingots, bars and sheets of steel	1·6	1·8	2·6	2·9	,,
Pig and puddled iron	2·5	2·3	3·0	3·6	,,
	£43	42	42	52	

Note 7.—Coal.

See pp. 108-111.—The exportation of coal has continued to increase rapidly.

QUANTITY OF COAL EXPORTED.

Average of years.	To Foreign Countries.	For use of steamers in foreign trade.
1880-84	20,100,000 tons	5,750,000 tons
1890-94	29,400,000 ,,	8,550,000 ,,
1900-04	44,100,000 ,,	14,900,000 ,,

The coal in the last column is not included in general statements of exports, but forms part of the expenses which, as cost of shipping and freights, go to pay for the excess of our imports; in addition, a part of the other column is accountable for by the needs of our ships abroad. The coal export trade, because of its bulk, is very important in providing cargoes for the out-journey for ships which bring home our imports. The value of coal exported was 10 per cent. of the total value of exports of home products in 1901-04. Though the output from the coalfields of Great Britain has increased steadily, it has been passed both by Germany and the United States. The South Wales coal has been in rapidly increasing demand abroad, and the question is often raised whether it is advisable to allow its export unchecked. An export duty of 1s. per ton has been in force on all coal since 1901. It has recently been alleged that the great importance of coal in our foreign trade was a sign of our weakness, and that we are exporting raw material and capital that cannot be replaced; in answer, it may be said that the great part of the cost of coal is due to labour, and that its export does not differ essentially in this respect from that of manufactured goods; and that the Royal Commission on Coal, which reported in January, 1905, gave reassuring accounts of the amount of coal still in the mines, so that the effects suggested on pages 108, 109 will be more remote than has been supposed. [See Mr. D. A. Thomas's paper, *Stat. Journal*, 1903, for a masterly discussion of the whole subject.]

Note 8.—SILVER.

See pp. 96-102.—The following table gives the price of silver and the exchange value of the rupee :—

	1890	1891	1892	1893	1894	1895	1896
Silver per oz. :	48d.	45d.	40d.	36d.	29d.	30d.	31d.
Rupee—Average rate of council bills :	16½d.	18d.	17d.	15d.	14½d.	13d.	14d.
	1897	1898	1899	1900	1901	1902	
Silver per oz. :	28d.	27d.	27d.	28d.	27d.	24d.	
Rupee—Average rate of council bills :	14½d.	15d.	16d.	16d.	16d.	16d.	

The price of silver, measured in gold, has thus continued to fall rapidly, but the value of the rupee has been kept up. The Indian regulations described on page 100 appear to have met with complete success ; the rupee fell a little after the closing of the mints to silver, but as the demand for it increased, it returned to 16d., and in 1899 the scheme was completed, and gold was declared legal tender in India ; since then silver in India is token money, 15 rupees representing a sovereign, though the silver contained in them is only worth about 12s. 6d. According to Mr. Robertson's paper, "The Currency Policy of India" (*Journal of the Society of Arts*, March, 1903), the measures have met with great success. India's trade with gold-using countries (estimated at three-fourths of the whole) is now on a stable basis. Many other countries have adopted a gold standard, Costa Rica in 1896, and Russia and Japan in 1897 ; the Straits Settlements and Peru have taken steps in the same direction. In the United States the purchase of silver arranged under the Sherman Act of 1890 was discontinued in 1893, and their currency system appears now to be firmly established on a gold basis.

Note 9.—RE-EXPORTS.

See Diagrams ix. and x., p. 135.—The numbers indicated in Diagram x. are those for Imports, whether for home consumption or re-export. Exports of Foreign and Colonial Produce (termed "re-exports") are valued at from £56 to £70 millions, or about one-seventh of total Imports annually in the period 1889-1903, the same fraction as in 1855-59.

QUINQUENNIAL AVERAGES.

	Imports.	Re-exports.	Exports of Home Produce,
1855-9	169,000,000	23,000,000	116,000,000
1860-4	235,000,000	42,000.000	138,000,000
1865-9	286,000,000	49,000,00	181,000,000
1870-4	346,000,000	55,000,000	235,000,000
1875-9	375,000,000	55,000,000	202,000,000
1880-4	408,000,000	64,000,000	234,000,000
1885-9	379,000,000	61,000,000	226,000,000
1890-4	419,000,000	62,000,000	234,000,000
1895-9	453,000,000	60,000,000	238,000,000
1900-4	533,000,000	67,000,000	281,000,000

The re-exports only give employment to shipping and transport agents. Raw cotton and wool accounted in 1895-99 for a yearly average of some £17,000,000; and these numbers have been subtracted in line C, Diagram ix., to give a correct view of the amount imported for home use. Other goods, which reach us in a partly manufactured state, are exported when finished, so that in reality our exports of "home produce" contain a considerable foreign element. Considerable sums should therefore be subtracted both from our imports and exports (*viz.*: the value of all imported raw materials and partly manufactured goods, which are manufactured and ultimately re-exported), before a correct view can be obtained of the importance of foreign trade to us. The materials for such a calculation do not exist.

Note 10.—SOURCES OF IMPORTS.

See Diagram x., p. 135.—The countries credited in the returns as supplying our imports are in many cases the countries of consignment, not of origin. Goods from Germany often come to us from Dutch or Belgian ports, and have been credited to those countries. Swiss and some Italian goods are credited to France or Belgium ; Austrian to Germany, Canadian to U.S.A., and *vice versâ*. The most important case is that of Germany, and a more correct view can be obtained by grouping together Germany, Holland, and Belgium ; or (for more general purposes) Germany, Russia, Austria, Holland, Belgium, Italy, Switzerland, and France. The trade accounts are, since 1st January, 1904, kept on both systems, showing country of consignment and that of origin. The differences between the two for the first half of 1904 are given in the Board of Trade memorandum, Cd. 2337, pp. 350-375.

FINIS.

INDEX.

(*No index other than page* viii. *is given to diagrams.*)

H

I

J

L

M

N

O

P

R

S

V

W

Y

Z

Printed by Cowan & Co., Limited, Perth.

For Product Safety Concerns and Information please contact our EU representative GPSR@taylorandfrancis.com
Taylor & Francis Verlag GmbH, Kaufingerstraße 24, 80331 München, Germany

www.ingramcontent.com/pod-product-compliance
Lightning Source LLC
LaVergne TN
LVHW011132300926
849160LV00008B/619

* 9 7 8 1 1 3 8 8 6 5 2 8 0 *